WHO SAYS GET MARRIED?

HOW TO BE HAPPY AND SINGLE

by

DON MEREDITH

THOMAS NELSON
Nashville

Published in Nashville, Tennessee, by Thomas Nelson, Inc., Publishers and distributed in Canada by Lawson Falle, Ltd., Cambridge, Ontario.

Printed in the United States of America.

Scripture quotations are from the New American Standard Bible, © The Lockman Foundation 1960, 1962, 1963, 1968, 1972, 1973, 1975, and are used by permission.

Library of Congress Cataloging in Publication Data

Meredith, Don.
  Who says get married?

  1. Single people. 2. Marriage—Moral and religious aspects. 3. Interpersonal relations. 4. Christian life—1960–   . I. Title.
BV835.M39   241'.63   81–16949
ISBN 0–8407–5741–7   AACR2

To the single friends
whom God has richly used
to enhance the lives
of Sally and me:

Ney Bailey
Randy Heady
Carol Wierman

and my sisters and brother,
Rosalie, Star, and Rock Meredith

Acknowledgments

Many people have had a part in this book. God's Spirit has graciously used many sources to help me communicate these thoughts.

Two single women in particular who have affected my life and this material are Ney Bailey and Carol Wierman. Sally and I consider these friends invaluable to us. We both look up to these women as godly models, and we want to express our thanks for their lives.

I want to thank the Family Ministry of Campus Crusade for Christ who first challenged me to present these thoughts at their Family and Singles Conferences.

I especially want to thank those men and women who have a "covenant" relationship with me and my wife Sally. Without them this material would be simply academic.

In conclusion, I would like to thank the Thomas Nelson publishing team for its continued support. Sandy Warden and Lisa Ferris have added much more than normal editing. They truly are a part of this book.

Contents

Foreword

This is the singles book for which we have all been waiting. Most people have a high view of marriage and a low view of being single. Or they have a high view of being single and a low view of marriage. Don Meredith has a high view of both because God has a high view of both.

Don, more than anyone I know, is able to present to us in simple, understandable terms God's ultimate view on relationships. He lifts us above the realm we live in and reveals God's viewpoint. He gives us hope in life, hope in viewing ourselves, hope in relationships. In short, this is a book of hope: hope in God and His Word.

I first learned the principles outlined in this book in 1973, and they changed my life. As I have continued to practice them, apply them to my life and teach others, I have found that they work.

You are in for a treat. Prepare to hear the truth in a way you may never have heard it before. Prepare to be encouraged, strengthened, helped. Prepare to hear the ultimate view of singleness.

Ney Bailey
National Traveling Representative
Campus Crusade for Christ

1
The Importance of Significance

Through a mutual friend, Debbie asked to see me. She had been experiencing a great deal of anxiety and fear since Richard, her present boy friend, had asked her to marry him. When she entered my office, I saw a very attractive and most feminine young lady in her late twenties. But one aspect of her disposition was immediately apparent; she was excessively burdened and depressed.

We had barely finished greeting one another when she burst into tears. The next hour was difficult for her, but gradually the facts became clear. A past romance was influencing Debbie's present life. After graduation from college she had fallen in love with a law student. They had dated during his three years of law school and had planned to marry after graduation. Those three years were difficult, filled with anxiety and struggle. The difficulties were amplified by the attitude of Debbie's mother, who continually opposed her decision to marry. The accompanying problems came to a head when her fiancé backed out just two weeks before the wedding. Debbie was embarrassed, embittered, and felt rejected.

The next two years were filled with emotional ups and downs. Subconsciously, Debbie took the broken relationship as a personal failure. She felt as if life had passed her by and there was nothing in the future to look forward to. She rejected her mother because of her "I told you so" attitude. Debbie began to fear relationships with men; yet she longed for the event she felt would alone undo her inner feelings of personal failure: marriage.

When Richard entered the scene, Debbie was a walking time bomb. On the surface, she was an attractive and seemingly successful career person. Yet, internally, she was a bag of nerves, her emotional life bogged down with introspection. Her actions reflected this internal drama.

She needed Richard desperately. Yet, she deeply feared he too would fall out of love. This emotional pressure actually blocked her conscious ability to know if she really loved him. We talked about Debbie's fears and needs at length that day but came to few solutions. I did not see her again until eighteen months later. Her roommate called me out of desperation to tell me that Debbie had not been able to overcome her internal struggles. In fact, the same cancellation of plans that had occurred with the law student was about to happen again. As much as he loved her, Richard could not go through with the engagement because of Debbie's volatile condition. Debbie was emotionally paralyzed, which confirmed in her mind that she was a failure.

I can identify to a degree with Debbie's all-consuming desire for marriage. In our American culture where marriage is often considered the "perfect" state, most single people must deal with feeling "different." Debbie's despair demonstrated just one of a number of possible responses to this cultural pressure to get married.

You may be saying that you certainly are not an unstable person who cannot give or receive love and intimacy from the opposite sex. But that's not the point. Debbie's dilemma began long before her engagement to the law student. Somewhere along the line, she was told, or she assumed, that *marriage is the key to a significant life*. That, of course, is just not true—but many Christians, both single and married, believe, either consciously or subconsciously, that it is true. This erroneous assumption then tragically becomes the basis for many important decisions, including career, life-style, church and social affiliations. Debbie was looking desperately for significance in life. To her, marriage was vital to that fulfillment.

People need to know that who they are and what they do has meaning, purpose, and lasting value. Without that knowledge, life is never satisfying and the search for significance never-ending.

If a person is married, he or she may think significance can be found only by being single again, free from the responsibilities of home and family. Often the person who never has married is equally certain that being significant is the same thing as being married. Some people try to feel significant by pursuing prestigious careers, accumulating wealth, earning degrees, even by outdoing others in their service for mankind. But where is true significance to be found? What really makes life meaningful?

These questions are ones that almost everyone, at some time, has grappled with. Single people are certainly no exception; and perhaps a case can be made that those who are not married often feel less significant than those who are happily married and raising a family.

Christians who are single (those for whom this book was written) may feel especially insignificant because of the emphasis on marriage and family within the church. Often single Christians are given the impression that to have a significant role in the church they must first marry (unless, of course, they want to be missionaries). Obviously, if this were true, Jesus, a single adult, couldn't be the Head of the church and Paul, who was also single, would have been out of order when he referred to himself as an apostle in the church.

So, who—or what—is saying you have to get married to be significant? Are you listening to the American culture or are you listening to God? Personal significance from God's perspective is not dependent upon marriage—or singleness, for that matter.

I challenge you to ask yourself the question, "What would I do with my life if I knew I would never marry?" Perhaps you would do exactly what you are doing now. But as you honestly consider that question, you may discover that you tune God out whenever He suggests a path that you feel will narrow your chances of finding a mate. If that's true, and you feel less than significant, then this book is for you. Consider with me these three affirmations:

1. Marriage is not the key to life.
2. Singles must develop lasting relationships.
3. Singles must be purposeful about their vocations and lives.

I am convinced that these three statements express the insight necessary for developing a dynamic life-style.

PART I

MARRIAGE IS NOT
THE KEY TO LIFE

2

Who Says Get Married?

My heart goes out to Debbie. But even though her life was painful, it was less painful than had she married Richard in her desperate, confused state.

Probably the most pathetic person I see in counseling is the individual who has been taught that marriage is the key to happiness in life and then, because of that belief, allows himself or herself to be pressured into marriage. After getting married, instead of a fantasy of blissful love, this person discovers that he or she is in an emotional box, which is being squeezed tighter and tighter. Marriage thus becomes "wedlock" instead of bliss. Anger, rejection, manipulation, and depression are the results.

Other Singles

Debbie's plight with marital pressure triggered an interest in me to discover how other singles respond to this cultural pressure to marry. Over the years since my encounter with Debbie I have observed many different responses to this pressure. Consider the following single people, who range in age from twenty-five to forty-five. Each one handles single life and the cultural pressure to marry a little differently.

David is one of the oldest and certainly the most mature single man I have ever met. His success is readily apparent. He is a respected accountant and is so stable and peaceable that he is known as a "big brother" to others. David knows that he will probably never marry and apparently is satisfied in his singleness. He is purposeful about both life and relationships; yet he does not have a deep desire for marriage. Basically he believes that since God has not given him a wife, he is better off being single and trusting God to take care of his needs.

Then there is Leslie, twenty-five, who, like David, seems satisfied being single. But unlike David, her satisfaction is probably only temporary. What is satisfaction at age twenty-five may well be frustration at twenty-seven or thirty-seven. In other words, Leslie's satisfaction is tied to a youthful desire to "experience life" before settling down into marriage.

Another is Cathy, who views single life and marriage much differently. An outspoken Christian, she deeply resents any implication that marriage is necessary or has any advantage over single life. She repeatedly recalls with some contempt pastors and married couples who have implied that it is best for singles to marry. At every lecture and seminar she attends, Cathy listens intently to perceive the speaker's attitude, almost hoping to hear some implication that marriage is necessary to happiness.

Ed stands out in my mind as a showcase extrovert. His life revolves around "making the scene." "Likable," "outgoing," and "personable" characterize him. I suspect that one of the most exhilarating aspects of life for Ed is capturing the attention of a female. The dating

scene gives him the feeling of acceptance and understanding that makes him feel like "number one."

Still another attitude toward single life and marriage is
communicated by Mack. He is thirty-two years old and is
neither embittered toward marriage nor seeking it. Instead, he is deeply confused about marriage. His past
experiences in relationships with women have not been
positive, and he is unsure why. He only knows that he
meant well but was unable to establish lasting friendships. Mack comes from a home where he observed the
embittered relationship of his divorced parents. That
experience left him fearful, and his persistent apprehen-
sion causes him to block the formation of deep relationships.

Judy represents yet another category of single people
today. She is one of the growing number of singles who
are ignored by the opposite sex because of the current
emphasis on external beauty. Judy has discovered over
time that, although solid friendships are available to her,
romance usually eludes her because of her not-so-pretty
appearance. The men she most admires avoid her for
reasons beyond her control. This is a tragic commentary
on the "beautiful people" mentality in the American
culture.

Jack is thirty-nine and divorced. He can visit his
children only occasionally. He has been divorced for four
years after ten years of marriage. The idea of marriage is
anxiety-producing for him. His marriage was one of
conflict, isolation, and disappointment. He is uncertain
about remarriage but will probably remarry someday for
the same reasons he married in the first place. Research
shows, however, that people like Jack who remarry
usually give up quickly when the second marriage en-

counters problems. Sixty percent of second marriages do not succeed.

New Perspective Long Overdue

As I think about these seven very different single people, I realize that the time for a new way of looking at remaining single is long overdue, especially within the church. After all, one out of three adults in this country is single. Statistics also indicate that the number of singles who never marry or who marry later in life is growing. A 1978 census bureau report stated that eleven percent of households are maintained by single persons who have never married, compared to seven percent in 1970. For whatever reason, people are choosing to remain single longer, and some are choosing never to marry. Many adults have become single again because of divorce or death of their spouse. The truth is, most adults will at one time or another be single for an indefinite period of time. So, learning to view being single as an acceptable, sometimes preferable, situation is essential to good mental and emotional health for everyone.

Given what both Jesus and Paul said about being married versus being single, the church should be in the forefront when it comes to encouraging the single lifestyle for those who will accept it. Something is sadly wrong with a church that pressures singles to marry and ignores those who choose to stay single.

If you're like me, you're asking the question, "Why all this pressure to get married?" Parents, pastors, churches, the media, the government, and virtually every focus of authority in America imply or state outright that marriage is the answer to loneliness. From birth, the programming is omnipresent.

We Americans are taught subtly that life is circumstantial. We are programmed to believe that joy and statisfaction in life will come in the next experience or the next fantasy of life. From our earliest years, our greatest joys in life are looking forward to our upcoming birthday, or Christmas, or a holiday. As we get older, we exist for athletics, summer vacations, and weekends. With the teen years come desires for popularity, a girl friend or boy friend, use of the car, and sexual discovery. Later still, the "missing link" of life becomes high school graduation, college and a car of our own.

After college, marriage is the next necessity in life—along with a career. Finally, owning a home, having children, and retiring fit into the pattern that is set in place from birth: the pattern for the good life and fulfillment. Certainly these things are good and part of a maturing and happy life, but be careful: They can also become a myth!

In other words, these experiences are not necessarily for every person. Society insists that you are not successful if you miss a step or two, but such programmed attainment is not all there is. Instead of facing life's circumstances bravely and wisely, some of us subconsciously or consciously believe that our problems will be solved if we can just get on to the next life experience, whether that be a new job, marriage, or retirement.

I am convinced that the major cause of "mid-life crisis" in America is that men and women in their forties have exhausted the myths of life. We are left with the reality that the secret to life is no longer hidden in the next experience. Most people, I believe, never fully recover from this shock, and they spend the rest of their life blaming others because they have missed life's best.

Marriage easily can be the biggest myth of all. (And I

say this as one who is sky high on the institution of marriage!) After puberty, most of us experience a little of the blessing and attraction of the opposite sex. The tender touch of a special person seems to heal our wounded souls and hungering emotions. Surely, we think, marriage must be the missing link to ultimate joy and happiness in life.

The American culture tolerates a single person's plight in life as normal until the mid-twenties. Then the culture calls for marriage. There are only small signs of rejection at first. But around age thirty, all the plugs of the culture are pulled. It shouts, "You're *different*! What's wrong with you?" Rejection's mouthpiece is normally parents, or churches, or friends—especially married friends. The escape of such rejection is sometimes thought to be found in singles groups: in bars, churches, apartment units, or clubs.

From the late twenties on, people who do not marry or who come from broken marriages enter, at best, a defensive period in life. The least demand that is placed on the most successful single is a constant explanation (sometimes spoken, sometimes unspoken) as to *why* they botched society's norm and have not married.

The most vocal confrontations, unfortunately, are initiated by people who are married. First, they are sorry that their single friend is relegated to the "second squad," the reserves of life. Since, in their minds, every normal, red-blooded American gets married, they are tempted to think one of two things: (1) This individual has a personality problem and cannot relate well enough to get married, or (2) he or she has homosexual tendencies. This is tragic! To attribute this prejudice to all married people would be unfair, but often such an attitude is revealed by even the most sensitive and caring couples. The result is tremendous pressure on single people to prove both to themselves and to their married friends that they are "normal." Single Christians, then, are forced either to resist such pressure until God provides a mate or to give in to it by marrying outside of God's will.

I recall talking to a Christian mother whose daughter had married a non-Christian. With utter sincerity she explained that there had been no Christian men her daughter's age in their small church and, therefore, her daughter had had no choice. The idea that her daughter could have and, indeed, should have remained single, trusting God for her needs, apparently had not occurred to this mother. Of course, even if she had taught her daughter that marrying unbelievers is outside God's will, her daughter might have chosen to do so anyway. But chances are good that the daughter had never been taught to look upon singleness positively, as an adventure and a blessing.

The singles mentioned earlier in this chapter are operating under the cultural pressure to marry, and they handle it in several different ways. In my experience, I have found there are six major responses to this cultural pressure.

1. The Satisfied Single

Let's start with the positive. More and more, I am encountering single people who have made a decision to remain single and are confident enough to announce, "Marriage is not for me, at least not for now." Their certainty and public declaration do two things. First, they set people at ease. Married people and singles alike enjoy being with singles who are comfortable with their status. Second, and most important, such confidence releases the single person to be purposeful,* successful, and to enjoy a sense of completeness in life. These singles are so relaxed they fit in almost anywhere.

2. The Desperate-for-marriage

This person is 180 degrees from the satisfied single and, like Debbie, would rather die than stay single. "Panic" is his or her byword. Such panic usually starts at an early age, perhaps because of an overly concerned mother who begins to push her child socially. Or maybe during puberty, the person assumes he or she is less attractive than other people physically, intellectually, or in personality. The result? Overcompensation and a desperate drive to be *accepted*. This person goes through life feeling that happiness will pass him by if he doesn't marry.

3. The Marriage Resentment Crowd

A growing group of singles resents any suggestion that marriage should be sought after. Considering the alternatives presented by our culture, I am not surprised. On closer examination, the real cause for resentment runs far deeper. One cause is hostility toward one or both parents, which results in hostility toward the opposite sex.

The other cause is lack of an adequate love model from either parent. People who have no model for love become fearful and unsure of themselves in dating rela-

---

*Throughout this book I will use *purposeful* as a catchword to denote an approach to life that is determined, creative, full of goals and ideals, and active as opposed to indifferent or hesitant.

tionships, especially as they approach marriage. These singles like someone at first but find it difficult to hold onto their feelings after dating for a while. This sets up a pattern of relationship failure which, later in life, causes them to be depressed and defensive.

4. Fear of Marriage

Increasingly in our culture, singles are apprehensive about marriage. The large number of secularly oriented singles who have decided to live together before marriage are, for the most part, afraid of making a lasting commitment. Many complain that they cannot take the marriage step, even though they feel love for the other person. Most singles know that more than forty percent of today's marriages eventually end in divorce. But there are other reasons they fear marriage. One reason is the lack of reassurance from successful marriages. Growing up, they saw few marriages that worked well. Past failure and rejection in personal relationships also adds to fear of lifetime commitment. Finally, singles are, in short, just not sure what makes marriage work.

5. Marriage Rejection

In the early years of childhood, we are told the fairy tales of Sleeping Beauty, Snow White, Cinderella, (along with sagas of great athletes for boys), all of which say beauty and strength are better. So we set out to be pretty or strong. While teachers respond to the intellectually sharp students, boy-crazy girls write love notes to physically attractive boys. Coaches respond to the physically strong boys, and outspoken students are elected to school offices. Finally, James Bond confirms that the beautiful, sexy, intelligent, athletic, and bold people get all the prizes.

I am counseling more and more singles who desire to marry but face constant rejection because they don't fit the mold set by the standards of our culture. The amazing thing is, usually the person I counsel is quite attractive but is rejected because he or she sets goals based solely on superficial standards: good looks, popularity, charm, poise, talent. Such people are guilty of judging their dating partner by the same ridiculous standards by which they are judged. Therefore, many times they pursue a person who may be programmed to reject them.

6. Marriage Failure

The last and fastest growing segment of singles who respond to the pressure to marry are those who have experienced marital failure previously. This category is made up of massive numbers of people who have failed once or twice in finding happiness or fulfillment in marriage. In fact, statistics say that ninety percent of those who have been married twice will never remarry. Divorce is a tragic event in any person's life; yet even more tragic is the fact that many who are divorced hurry to remarry. If marriage is not the key to life, then certainly remarriage is not either. Divorced singles need to look for fulfillment of their needs through ways other than marriage.

Which response to the pressure to marry best describes your own? Are you satisfied being single? Or do you feel rejected and fearful? Perhaps you have failed at marriage and find yourself confused and discouraged about the future.

You may be saying, "Okay, so marriage isn't the key to a significant life. I still have needs that can only be met by other people, and sometimes only by the opposite sex." Before reading ahead to see how to meet those needs outside of marriage take time to consider what *is* the key to life.

3

The Key to Life

Recently, I asked a group of single Christians to list the three experiences they considered most important to happiness. The responses did not vary. A successful marriage was always at the top of the list. The distant second was a toss-up among successful career, children, and security.

If you were asked to list life's most important ingredients, what would your response be? The answer is crucial, for if you answer incorrectly you will miss what life is all about. I've already stated that marriage is not the ultimate experience or the guarantee to fulfillment and significance. Let me illustrate why.

I am tremendously excited about marriage, and my greatest earthly blessings are my wife, Sally, and our children. But marriage in and of itself is not the proverbial pot at the end of the rainbow. As a newlywed, I was shocked to discover that there is very little automatic blessing in marriage.

I naively assumed, for example, that marriage would automatically remove my occasional, deep sense of loneliness. Surely having a wife would insure never being alone in life's despairing moments. Much to my surprise, after our honeymoon was over, I experienced one of the loneliest points in my life. I went through a period of uncertainty regarding my vocational strengths. Sally's presence was of little help. She was actually a slight discouragement because of her lack of understanding and knowledge of my vocational strengths and was occasionally judgmental. Only God brought me comfort at this lonely point in my life. Before long, I began to see that every fear and concern I had when I was single was still present after I married.

God never says that being married is better than being single. (We will look at this truth in detail in Chapter 4.) So, if marriage is not the key to happiness, what is? Let me share with you a clear statement of God's key to happiness and life.

Knowing God

There is *nothing* more important than knowing God. Jesus said, "'This is eternal life, that they may know Thee, the only true God, and Jesus Christ whom Thou hast sent'" (John 17:3), and "'. . . I came that they might have life, and might have it abundantly'" (John 10:10). Marriage and all else become unimportant issues when contrasted with the desire to experience abundant life here and eternal life after death. So you see, the real issue is, Do you know God?

You may be saying, "Yes, I know God. I'm a Christian. But I'm still dissatisfied being single." Okay. Being dissatisfied with your life occasionally is normal, but where you look for satisfaction is crucial. Continual discontent is a sign of an inner need, a need only God can satisfy. Paul said he could be content in whatever situation he found himself, and Paul was single. Do you *want* to be content while you're single? If so, then begin to take stock of your spiritual life and your relationship with Jesus Christ. How well do you know Him? Be honest.

Are there barriers between you and Jesus? Is your time being used the way He wants you to use it?

There are many biblical passages that state God's key to life clearly. Let's concentrate here on 2 Peter 1:2–11, where God reveals through Peter what constitutes a mature and godly person who has discovered the key to life.

> Grace and peace be multiplied to you in the knowledge of God and of Jesus our Lord; seeing that His divine power *has granted to us everything pertaining to life and godliness*, through the true knowledge of Him who called us by His own glory and excellence. For by these He has granted to us His precious and magnificent promises, in order that by them you might become partakers of the divine nature, having escaped the corruption that is in the world by lust (2 Pet. 1:2–4; italics mine).

What is the key to life? Peter clearly states that "everything pertaining to life and godliness" is granted to us through a knowledge of God. Notice Peter says *everything*. Grace, peace, happiness, relationships, security, emotional needs, sexual needs—*everything* that is important to life and godliness comes from a knowledge of God. The word *knowledge* means full, *personal*, and accurate knowledge of God. Peter is not talking about a degree in theology here. He's talking about an intimate and practical, daily relationship with God.

At this point, we are faced with an idea that conflicts with our culture and human instinct. The philosophy behind the statement "If it feels good, do it" does not compute with Peter's suggestion. Peter says that a dynamic life is not found by seeking sex, marriage, wealth, or prestige; instead, life is found in a personal knowledge of God.

Any single person who dares to override his or her

human instincts and who seeks to know God through Jesus Christ will not be unfulfilled. Life will be full to overflowing. This fact becomes clear at the reunion of old friends. A group of singles I knew twelve years ago met together recently. Whether single or married today, there was a noticeable difference in the current outlooks of the group. After several days of interaction, the evidence was overwhelming: Those people whose lives were anchored in seeking after God were experiencing more dynamic lives. Their outlook on the future was unbelievably better.

Peter further equates life with godliness. *Godliness* comes from a word that means reverence. Webster defines *reverence* as "profound adoring and awed respect." What better way to gain knowledge and life than through adoration and respect of God?

Godliness seems old-fashioned and outmoded to some, even to a number of so-called Christians. But to the single who has found contentment, godliness is life itself. A single friend of mine is forever taking the time to get alone to pray and study God's Word: a few minutes at a local park, a couple of hours set aside in her schedule. She constantly seeks contact with God. So, I am not surprised when I constantly hear people say, "There's something different and attractive about her life." The godliness in her life far outshines any marriage I have seen.

Singles, now is the time to strike a blow for life! Transfer your hope in life from dreams of marriage to God. Believe His Word. Settle your allegiance today, choosing life and godliness by seeking to know God.

For years I pursued life's myths, each leaving me desolate, only to see that my human goals, apart from God, bring nothing of lasting value. But as I seek God and His will, He graciously gives me many of my human goals; not because I deserve them or have earned them, but because He loves me.

Peter goes on to say that in this knowledge of God and His Word, we are given certain "precious and magnificent promises." These promises breed hope and give us God's power to defeat the world system that sidetracks us from true happiness. Promises from God's Word alone offer reality and hope. I meet people daily who have "done it my way." Many people, single and married, seek to gratify themselves by manipulating people, using people, overpowering people, stealing from people, worshiping people, and being controlled by people. God's Word promises a better way, a way that is good, healthy, and overflowing with peace. What excitement when a person discovers that God's promises are true and practical.

Last year Jim was caught in a terrible worldly web. An attractive, intellectual woman wanted to marry him. Her only weakness was her resentment of Jim's Christianity. She gave him an ultimatum: "Christianity or me!" Jim died a little emotionally and suffered a lot, but he chose to let his heart's desire pass as he chose Christianity. This year Jim's heart is repaired, and his life is a joy.

A Mindset of Faith

> Now for this very reason also, applying all diligence, in your faith supply moral excellence, and in your moral excellence, knowledge;
> and in your knowledge, self-control,
> and in your self-control, perseverance,
> and in your perseverance, godliness;
> and in your godliness, brotherly kindness,
> and in your brotherly kindness, Christian love
> (2 Pet. 1:5–7).

A knowledge of God is our hope for life and godliness. But we must respond to God with faith. What kind of faith? Faith rooted in a knowledge of God, the kind that adheres to His promises whether they make sense or not. Faith is demonstrated when we do what God says instead of following our human instinct. Doing what faith requires is different from the normal human response, because the divine nature is utterly different from human nature. But what could be more fulfilling than experiencing, through faith, God's own nature? What better way to know Him?

Moral Excellence

Peter says our first step of obedient faith should result in being committed to moral excellence. The word *moral* means intrinsic moral goodness, as in speaking of a virtue of God. Why do you think moral excellence comes before knowledge?

The most basic step of faith a person can make is beginning a personal relationship with God through faith in Jesus Christ. Are we willing to choose God's moral perspective over our own? Is God for real? Is He trying to get us to "try" religion or can we know God on a moment-by-moment practical basis? Does only a practical knowledge of Him really give life? To find success in life, one must first determine that only God and His way works. Are you willing to believe God? Or are you going to believe in yourself?

You see, moral excellence is costly. We are called to turn our backs on the fleeting pleasures of sin. Every single is faced with the choice of fleeting pleasure or lasting pleasure through a moral commitment to God and His perspective concerning life. Do the pleasures of this world work over the long haul, or does a knowledge of God and His perspective work better?

There is no hope for the person who lives only for momentary pleasures. Millions of empty lives prove that fact. If God's call to moral excellence sounds legalistic to you, believe me, your knowledge of God is faulty. God hates sin for a reason: It destroys those who practice it and who refuse to stop. Moral excellence involves our body, soul, and spirit or, put another way, our body, emotions, and deeds.

Knowledge

Once you begin to seek earnestly for God's moral excellence, your knowledge of God and His ways will increase. You will begin to understand better why moral excellence is required, and your trust in the Source of true knowledge will grow. The word *knowledge* used here refers to investigating truth, especially spiritual truth. God promises that the single who seeks after God's perspective will be rewarded with knowledge that comes only from God. This knowledge is the knowledge that results in everything pertaining to life. The longer a person keeps God's perspective and discovers this truth, the more satisfied with life he or she will be.

Self-Control

Why do people panic and make confused and hasty decisions? The reason is related to their lack of wisdom or knowledge about what to do. As God's knowledge concerning life grows in our hearts and minds we will through that knowledge become more self-controlled. I only panic when I am fearful and lose perspective or run out of alternatives. With God's perspective, self-control is a natural by-product.

Perseverance

In a culture where over half our hospital beds are filled with people who have given up coping with life, a Christian who perseveres in commitment to God's perspective is rare. Webster defines *perseverance* as persisting in spite of opposition. Perseverance is prolonged self-control. As one discovers God's knowledge, self-control results. As self-control verifies the practical truth of God's knowledge, continued self-control leads to perseverance in spite of opposition. A single who is able to persevere in God's perspective already is demonstrating a life-style that is distinguished from the typical life.

Godliness

The word Peter uses for *godliness* means reverence of God, both in attitude and action. A single who perseveres in his or her reverence of God will be called godly in this world. Maintaining God's perspective and persevering in one's knowledge of God over a period of time characterizes one's life as godly.

Brotherly Kindness

Most people's lives are characterized by mild panic; they are not able to persevere in anything. Therefore, they cannot persevere in their service and faithfulness toward people because of their own fears and struggles. People in panic cannot give to others but are only able to use others. For this reason love in today's world is very fickle.

Peter shocks us a bit by adding *brotherly kindness* to this "spiritual progress list." The words used imply "acts of brotherly love towards others." What Peter is saying is that only people who are persevering in self-control in their own lives are going to have the ability to be honestly aware of the needs of others. Peter is giving us a tremendous hint of how God's love differs from the world's.

Love

Every single person who rejects God and His perspective of life does so out of fear of missing something exciting in life. Usually we reject God for some human relationship, thinking that God's way will isolate us from love and intimacy. The irony of rejecting God is that no lasting relationship is possible apart from Him.

The greatest blessing for the single who chooses God and His perspective is the potential for lasting relationships. The word used here for love is *agape*, the word that describes God's love. God's love is not selfish but totally sacrificial. The single who rejects God and His perspective will never know the totally exhilarating life of loving and having been loved by God. The alternative is tragically inferior and short-lived.

Oh, to develop God's love as a way of life! But let me repeat it again: Getting married does not guarantee one's receiving love. True love only comes as we make a decision to live life God's way and to seek to know Him. Peter promises that the person who decides to seek a knowledge of God will live a significant life.

> For if these qualities are yours and are increasing, they render you neither useless nor unfruitful in the true knowledge of our Lord Jesus Christ (2 Pet. 1:8).

Make Certain of His Calling

> For he who lacks these qualities is blind or short-sighted,
> having forgotten his purification from his former sins.
> Therefore, brethren, be all the more diligent to make
> certain about His calling and choosing you; for as long as
> you practice these things, you will never stumble; for in
> this way the entrance into the eternal kingdom of our
> Lord and Savior Jesus Christ will be abundantly supplied
> to you (2 Pet. 1:9–11).

Peter concludes his statements on how to find life with
a warning: ". . . make certain about [God's] calling. . . ." If you profess to be a Christian but are compla-
cent about your relationship with God, and if your
attitude toward what He says in the Bible is one of
scornful skepticism, then you had better consider
whether you really are a Christian. Some of you may
realize you don't have a personal relationship with Jesus
Christ. If that's the case, then let me take this opportunity to introduce you to Him, through His own words
found in the Gospel of John. (I encourage you to read
John in its entirety, asking God to give you understanding.)

Jesus said, " 'Truly, truly, I say to you, unless one is
born again, he cannot see the kingdom of God' " (John
3:3). How is one born again? "For God so loved the
world, that He gave His only begotten Son, that whoever
believes in Him should not perish, but have eternal life"
(John 3:16). Jesus also said, " 'I am the way, and the
truth, and the life; no one comes to the Father, but
through me' " (John 14:6).

Sometimes a person's initial response to Christ's saying "I am the way" is negative because he or she views
God as rigid. The heart of God is not rigid. Instead, He
tells us the straight truth, motivated by deep love and

sacrifice for us. Christ demands that we come to the Father through Him because there simply is no other way.

In Romans 3:23 we read, "For all have sinned and [keep falling] short of the glory of God." God knows well what we are like inside. "But God demonstrates His own love toward us, in that while we were yet sinners Christ died for us" (Rom. 5:8). If you are burdened by guilt because of unconfessed sin and an unwillingness to admit your need for God's forgiveness through Jesus Christ, turn now to the Lord Jesus and pour out your heart to Him. If you aren't sure how to pray, perhaps the following prayer will help you:

> Jesus, forgive my sinful life. I turn from my old ways and thank You for dying for my sins. I accept Your death on the cross on my behalf as the payment that will allow me to know God. Come into my life right now as my Savior and Lord. Enable me to submit to You as Lord in each area of my life. Thank You for coming into my life. Amen.

Remember: "As many as received Him, to them He gave the right to become children of God, even to those who believe in His name" (John 1:12), and "If you confess with your mouth Jesus as Lord, and believe in your heart that God raised Him from the dead, you shall be saved" (Rom. 10:9).

In Conclusion

Is marriage the key to life? Does the married person have an advantage in life over the single? Certainly not. For the key to life is aggressively seeking the will of God through an intimate knowledge of Him.

The most important point of the passage in 2 Peter is

that life is in God. We can know God only if we come to Him on His terms by acknowledging our sinfulness and receiving His Son Jesus as our Lord. Marriage or singleness is an issue of calling, but a meaningful life is found in the knowledge of God. A single person obviously can know God every bit as well as a married person, and sometimes better. Therefore, both can have an equally fulfilling life. God may or may not call you to marriage but be assured that He has called you to experience abundant life, for Jesus said, " '. . . I came that [you] might have life, and might have it abundantly' " (John 10:10).

4

Four Crucial Questions

Many people are like boats dead in the water: no power, no plan, no vision, just floating, moved along by the currents of life. The proverb says, "Where there is no vision, the people perish . . ." (Prov. 29:18 KJV). Single people who fit this description must snap out of their daze and make decisions and commitments and begin to attack life aggressively. Fundamental to this aggressiveness is a solid trust that God is able to meet their deepest needs.

In that light, let's look at four questions that are crucial to living what I call an aggressive, Christian, single life.

1. What Can I Expect Immediately If I Dare to Believe God?

Many people are frustrated about being single because their every activity is controlled by the possibilities of social encounters. Many vocational, intellectual, and spiritual opportunities are ignored for fear of limiting one's chances of finding a mate. People who allow themselves to be controlled by fear (or their social calendar) often are frustrated and depressed. They are no longer living and growing; rather they are waiting for someone who may never show up. No doubt they want to marry someone who is excited about life and who knows how to love others. Will a person like that want to marry someone who is so hung up about being single that they have stopped growing spiritually, mentally, and emotionally? The people who have marriage in their thoughts constantly need to force themselves to focus on the concerns of others. They need to let God worry about their future mate while they get on with a life of service.

There are benefits of being single that are lost or restricted after marriage. A good example is the freedom to change and adjust to life's opportunities. Just recently a single woman in her early thirties was able to adjust her vocational direction in life at a time when it would have been impossible for a married person. The change will bring significant blessings and increased productivity for a lifetime. Another example is mobility and flexibility. A single person can move and take advantage of ministerial and educational opportunities that marriage greatly restricts. A single person can experience far greater expression of his or her spiritual gifts, generally speaking, than a married person.

A final illustration is the unencumbered spiritual growth afforded a single. Before I married, me plus God was a majority. If God was teaching me something, I was free to learn and respond immediately. Now, there are five other people (my wife and children) who also must respond to what God may be calling me to do. A single who has established lasting friendships but still has independence in the Lord has potentially the best of both worlds. Hard to believe, maybe, but true.

Trusting God with your singleness allows you both to

look to the future and to live for God in a vital way *now*. You no longer need to wait to be equipped for service and success. As you begin to function in full expression of your goals and priorities, you are much more likely to meet people with similar interests and values heading toward the same goals. The very person God may have for you will not recognize your gifts and values if you lack vision and direction.

To choose a purposeful single life is infinitely more satisfying than following the masses by setting marriage as your hope. To choose life whose hope is God gives you the best of both worlds. First, to believe God for a satisfying life insures total expression of yourself and your gifts if marriage never comes. But second, it also communicates an attractive life-style that insures attracting the opposite sex if God so chooses. A few days ago two single friends of mine were married. Both were approximately forty years of age. I believe they will truly have the best of both experiences; before they married they were successful singles. Even their married friends were concerned initially that marriage might be a letdown, because they were so dynamic and successful apart from one another. God is the key to their life, not marriage or being single.

As you begin to trust God, you will be free to let people know that, for now, singleness is God's choice for you. That simple declaration protects your commitment to and dependence on God. It implies tremendous stability, maturity, and availability to God and to others. Ultimately it frees other people from secretly evaluating your motives for staying single. As you develop godly relationships, you become an emotionally complete person of stature and attractiveness.

2. What If Marriage Never Comes?

For most people who put their hopes in the circumstantial issue of marriage, having to remain single
results in continual discouragement. Yet, many who
marry—thus experiencing their dream come true—soon
feel they "missed out" on life because they married too
young or married the wrong person. Again we learn that
marriage of itself is not the answer!

The single person who is seeking to know God discovers life on a totally different economy. God's system
of values puts a special blessing on the single. Does that
surprise you? God made a promise that all singles should
draw upon.

> . . . Neither let the eunuch [single] say, "Behold, I am a
>   dry tree."
> For thus says the LORD,
> "To the eunuchs who keep My sabbaths,
> And choose what pleases Me,
> And hold fast My covenant,
> To them I will give in My house and within My walls a
>   memorial,
> And a name better than that of sons and daughters;
> I will give them an everlasting name which will not be
>   cut off" (Is. 56:3–5).

This prophetic expression of God's view and commitment to singles is astounding! God clearly states that
being single is not useless, unfruitful, or unimportant.
To believe such things is *sin*! If a single faithfully follows
the will of God and perseveres in His way, God will bless
that person in a special way. I believe what God promises for eternity He begins to do in this lifetime. Paul
wrote:

But I say to the unmarried and to widows that it is *good* for them if they remain even as I (1 Cor. 7:8; italics mine).

But I want you to be *free from concern*. One who is unmarried is concerned about the things of the Lord, how he may please the Lord; but one who is married is concerned about the things of the world, how he may please his wife, and his interests are divided. And the woman who is unmarried, and the virgin, is concerned about the things of the Lord that she may be holy both in body and spirit; but one who is married is concerned about the things of the world, how she may please her husband. And this I say *for your own benefit*; not to put a restraint upon you, but to promote what is seemly, and to secure undistracted devotion to the Lord (1 Cor. 7:32–35; italics mine).

Jesus was not silent regarding the advantages of remaining single. One day a group of Pharisees was trying to test Jesus' orthodoxy, and they asked Him if it was lawful to divorce one's wife. (Divorce was frequent in those days, too.) Jesus said that according to Scripture a man and his wife become one flesh and that to separate "what God has joined together" would be wrong. The questioners immediately asked why Moses, then, allowed divorce. Jesus said Moses allowed it because of the hardness of people's hearts. In other words, the people refused to obey God and since Moses couldn't force them to obey, he allowed them to divorce.

The disciples understood exactly what Jesus was saying: To please God a man must live with the woman God gives him for life. They had no lofty illusions about marriage, not these twelve! Listen to their response: "'If the relationship of the man with his wife is like this, it is better not to marry'" (Matt. 19:10). Does Jesus set them straight, telling them that marriage is an experience no one should miss? Read on:

> "There are eunuchs who were born that way from their mother's womb; and there are eunuchs who were made eunuchs by men; and there are also eunuchs who made themselves eunuchs for the sake of the kingdom of heaven. He who is able to accept this, let him accept it" (Matt. 19:12).

In light of these words of Scripture, then, and the lives of the single men who said them, I believe more single Christians should be in leadership positions in the church. Christian couples—pastors and wives included—should recognize God's special blessing on their unmarried brothers and sisters. Single Christians need to be especially encouraged to develop their spiritual gifts and to use them in God's service. I'm not saying the church should take advantage of single people's time, giving them the jobs no one else wants to do. Rather, the attitude within the church toward singles should be one of encouragement and respect, not of sympathy and prejudicial disregard. Many of us who are married could stand to sit under the testimony of a mature single Christian whose devotion to the Lord is undistracted, especially since Paul exhorts married people to live as if they were single in terms of their devotion to God (see 1 Cor. 7:29ff).

The single men and women who heroically served Jesus Christ in His church throughout history are literally too numerous to name. The single Christian today who is purposeful in God's will and who is received and accepted in the church is unlimited in potential accomplishment and significance.

Paul and Jesus encouraged singles to remain single

and serve the Lord. They were not down on marriage, but they knew the potential problems that married people must face and work through. This was true in the first century; it is true today. The issue that is most vital to a fulfilled life is one of a personal knowledge of God and service for Him.

If you're worried that you may never marry, the scriptural exhortation to remain single may not be what you want to hear. Probably you want some assurance that you will marry eventually. All I can say is, if you're single now and your all-consuming desire is to be married, examine your motives. If you want marriage as a means to spiritual and emotional fulfillment, be careful. No other human can fully satisfy those needs. However, if you are truly unable to accept being single, if your sexual passions are nearly uncontrollable and keeping you from godly pursuits, then by all means ask God for a mate. Just tell Him you either need a mate or a drastic change in attitude and sexual desire. He *will* meet your needs one way or the other.

3. Does Knowing and Serving God *Really* Offer Fulfillment?

Fulfillment is the crucial question, isn't it? Paul declared his satisfaction with life not long before he was martyred: "I have fought the good fight, I have finished the course, I have kept the faith" (2 Tim. 4:7).

Does that sound like a frustrated single at the end of his life who is bitter over not being married, having children, or owning a home? Certainly not! Paul's "wife and children" were his disciples. His home was the church he helped build. He knew the exhilaration of knowing Christ, the very One who created him to be all that he was.

After counseling hundreds of both single and married people, I can say that anyone whom God calls to remain single is not only blessed but has a better chance of serving God in an unencumbered manner. God certainly has not shortchanged him!

> Have this attitude in yourselves which was also in Christ Jesus, who, although He existed in the form of God, did not regard equality with God a thing to be grasped, but emptied Himself, taking the form of a bond-servant, and being made in the likeness of men. And being found in appearance as a man, *He humbled Himself* by becoming obedient to the point of death, even death on a cross. Therefore also *God highly exalted Him*, and bestowed on Him the name which is above every name, that at the name of Jesus every knee should bow, of those who are in heaven, and on earth, and under the earth, and that every tongue should confess that Jesus Christ is Lord, to the glory of God the Father (Phil. 2:5–11; italics mine).

If Christ can be obedient to the Father to the point of becoming a bondservant through taking on our humanity, surely He can ask you to trust and obey Him for earthly fulfillment. Just as Christ was limited only temporarily by His life on earth and His death, so you need be limited only temporarily by your struggles as a single. Deal with each struggle on the spot! Humble yourself before your heavenly Father, and He will handle your need, lift you up, and glorify Christ through you. Realize that all God requires of you is a willingness to allow Him to work in your life and an openness to His will. Even a mustard seed of faith will grow!

4. Will You Be Purposeful?

Will you set aside your questions, your resentments, your self-pity, your stubborn self-will, your panic, your unbelief, and today choose to look to God alone for abundant life? Talk to Him, read His Word, and ask Him to give you a vision of where your life should be heading. Ask Him what He wants you to do today and each day with the time and talents He has given you. Ask Him for the peace that passes understanding so that you are no longer restless and anxious.

Self-acceptance, relationships, productivity, and social expression are vital to your life. But true life starts by asking God for the faith to trust and obey Him, to place your hope in Him, right now, just as you are. You need not wait! The resources are yours *now*.

God is not asking you to stick your little toe over the line of commitment. He is asking you to step across the line with your whole being. Believe God for your future. Doing so will make the difference between a meaningful life and a mediocre one.

PART II

DEVELOPING
LASTING RELATIONSHIPS

5

Who Needs You, Anyway?

Prominent best describes the older gentleman who entered my office some years ago. He was definitely what you would call a pillar of his community. His name was on the cornerstone of at least ten public buildings. His wealth was whispered about at social gatherings, and he had been the chairman of almost every major charitable fund drive in the city. As I sat visiting with this man in my office, I was deeply conscious of his public importance. Seemingly, he had accomplished everything life could offer.

Because he was twice my age, I was somewhat surprised that he was in my office for counseling. I had met him at several social gatherings but had no idea he knew my name. The first thirty minutes were spent just getting acquainted.

Finally, I broke the pleasantries and asked why he had come to see me. He told me that after his semi-retirement two years before, he and his wife of fifty years had separated. What pain and disappointment this man was experiencing! His heart was broken, and he was deeply hurt. After what most would consider a superb career, he was at the loneliest point in his life. There was no one to spend time with him.

I inquired about his children, but he said he couldn't communicate with them.

"How about the grandchildren?"

"Oh, they're all right . . . but . . . "

"Business acquaintances?"

"Well, no."

After seventy years of life, this man had numerous acquaintances, power, respect, but no real friends. Many would cry at his funeral because he had done a lot of nice things with his money. Yet, not one person would miss him in the middle of the day, a week after he was gone!

Do you see the point? There is something terribly wrong about buying into a system that deceives people with empty promises all through life. After years of being deceived, one day people realize that they have never established a lasting, intimate relationship with anyone. This particular man would have rated an A plus on the surface issues of life. Yet he was not intimate, in the deepest sense of the word, with even one person. How could this have happened?

Relationships are made, not found or stumbled upon! If people do not have an aggressive plan for relationships, they can expect to lose. John the apostle made a significant comment on the subject when he said, "We know that we have passed out of death into life, because we love the brethren. He who does not love abides in death" (1 John 3:14). The greatest evidence of a satisfying life, presently and eternally, is the demonstrated love we have for one another. People need relationships!

Many singles are not yet caught in a mistaken or impossible situation concerning relationships. They still have opportunities to beat the system that trapped the prominent businessman. But we are all enslaved in a

culture that sets numerous enticing traps around relationships. I'm afraid these traps are laid out at the very
time in life when we are most emotionally and sexually
vulnerable.

Tragically, mistakes made in the area of relationships
affect lives longer and more profoundly than any other
type of mistake. But successful, supportive relationships
established early in life can be the springboard to a more
productive life overall.

In the first part of this book we decided that a personal
knowledge of God is the most vital issue in life. Join with
me as we test that premise to see how God offers insight
into relationships.

How Important Are Relationships?

A young boy had been lost in the wilds of the Rockies
for three days and two nights. He was scratched and
bruised from head to foot. His body ached all over, half
from shock, half from the intensity of the early morning
chill.

His eyes stared into space with little sign of life, his
pupils never wavering, and his breathing was difficult
—a sad, wheezing noise. When rescuers found him they
covered him with a blanket and made every attempt to
communicate with him, but to no avail.

From somewhere off in the distance came the faint
sound of an approaching jeep. The vehicle screeched
to a halt and a woman screamed, "David! David!" The
frightened mother ran with abandon to grab her son. It
was as if she had lost her own life, but now had found it.
She held him close to her body, then madly but tenderly

began to search him, assuring herself that no part was missing.

Within moments, David's eyes focused and he began to cry. In broken, gasping phrases, he recounted the story of his frightening three days.

This story, taken from a newspaper account, illustrates powerfully the need for love in the human life. Isolation kills. Touch, concern, tears, and commitment show love. The need for human love is nonnegotiable.

Does God care whether or not you are loved by someone other than Him? Of course He does. God created relationships as the vehicle for love in the first place. His relationship with you was important enough to Him to send His Son to die for your sins. In fact, relationships are so important that He instructed the apostle John to make this statement, "If someone says, 'I love God,' and hates his brother, he is a liar; for the one who does not love his brother whom he has seen, cannot love God whom he has not seen" (1 John 4:20).

God realized that only through human relationships can we ever learn to respond to His love. Without human love, God's love cannot be fully understood or experienced in this life. To prepare properly for successful relationships, this truth must be firmly grasped: *God is the author of relationships.*

Humankind today is still making the mistake Lucifer made. Lucifer rejected dependence upon the all-wise God and decided he could live without God. We, too, depend on our own strength and wisdom for life instead of depending on God. As we discussed in the first part of the book, God-dependence is the key to life, not self-dependence. But even before the Fall, God created the earth—and human relationships—to demonstrate that only dependence on Him will bring life. Relationships are closely connected to God's purpose for creation.

Three Purposes for Humankind

Genesis 1 gives the account of how God created the heavens, the earth, animals, and, finally, humankind. In verses 26 through 28, God states three major purposes for humankind, and all three of these purposes are tied to relationships.

1. *Reflection of God's Image*
God's first purpose for humankind and relationships is stated in verses 26 and 27:

> Then God said, "Let Us make man in Our image, according to Our likeness; and let them rule over the fish of the sea and over the birds of the sky and over the cattle and over all the earth, and over every creeping thing that creeps on the earth." And God created man in His own image, in the image of God He created him; male and female He created them.

The first purpose of humankind is to reflect God's image on earth. The plural pronouns refer to the wholeness or trinity of God. In other words, God made humankind in His likeness so the world could see God.

The Scripture also implies that it takes both a man and a woman to reflect God's image. "Let *them* rule" means that isolated individuals cannot fulfill God's first purpose. Men and women must join together in relationships in order to reflect God's image. Marriage and the church are the two institutions that God created to accomplish this first purpose.

2. *Reproducing After Our Kind*

The second purpose of humankind is given in the first half of verse 28:

> And God blessed them; and God said to them, "Be fruitful and multiply, and fill the earth. . . . "

After creating Adam and Eve for the purpose of reflecting God's image on earth, God equipped and commanded them to reproduce His image by having godly children. Since this reproduction has marriage in view, how do we relate this command to single people? It is here that Christian service enters the picture. Singles, free from many normal family responsibilities, can direct their attention to bringing *spiritual* children into the family of God. They can reproduce disciples of Christ with similar rewards and results experienced by married people with earthly children. The church is vital relationally to singles.

3. *Reigning Upon Earth*

The third purpose of humankind is revealed in the last half of verse 28:

> " . . . subdue it [the earth]; and rule over the fish of the sea and over the birds of the sky, and over every living thing that moves on the earth."

God intends that men and women, working together, be strong and effective authorities on the earth. Therefore, God desires that men and women, whether married or single, together in the church, assist Him in leading the earth to dependence upon Christ for life and happiness.

We are to reflect God's image, reproduce godly children or disciples, and rule over the earth for God. God's purposes are clear. Thus, all Christian people, single or married, are important to God's purposes. And all of us must admit our need for relationships before we can fulfill God's plan.

The Body of Christ—The Church

The prototype of perfect relationships in Genesis is Adam and Eve—marriage. In the New Testament, this model is expanded *beyond* marriage:

> But now God has placed the members, each one of them, in the body, just as He desired. . . . And the eye cannot say to the hand, "I have no need of you"; or again the head to the feet, "I have no need of you" (1 Cor. 12:18,21).

Paul was talking about the church. Christ places each person in the church according to His desire, just as parts of the human body—head, hands, feet—are put together. Our interpersonal relationships in the church are so vital from God's perspective that He has knit us together as permanently and integrally as He formed the parts of our bodies.

This verse demonstrates that all believers are dependent on relationships outside of marriage. Single or married, people are incomplete without Christ-centered relationships. In the Body of Christ, we experience God's love in the deepest sense.

God has a plan. That plan is to demonstrate Christ's love to humankind by calling out a group of people—the church—who love one another. As our needs are met in the church, we will be enabled to share God's love with a lost world by reflecting God's image, to reproduce that image in children and disciples, and to reign with Christ over God's creation when He returns. Satan's self-dependence is exposed as folly when compared to the gracious sufficiency of God's love and provision for humankind.

Single, God is concerned that you have deep and lasting relationships, not just because He is God, but because *He created that need in you*. He knows you are incomplete in terms of your purpose, as well as His, without being knit together in satisfying relationships.

If you will continue to seek after a knowledge of Him, He will give you everything pertaining to life and godliness—including meaningful relationships. God is *the* author and creator of relationships. Therefore, our task is simply to recognize the relationships God has created for us, and to commit ourselves to them. How to do this is the topic of the next six chapters.

6

Relationships:
The World's Way

"Sure, Don, I'll tell you flat out what I did to the little creep," Barbara literally screamed at me.

"I started by taking every possession she owns, and I threw them in a pile by the front door. Then I sat down and wrote a letter to her fiancé and told him what a shock he was in for if he married her. Then I called the pastor to warn the church what little 'two-face' is up to."

I couldn't believe my ears. It seemed that just yesterday I had run into Barbara and Kathy after church and had been impressed by their excitement over the possibility of sharing an apartment together. I remembered thinking, "Those girls are really solid people. They'll make a strong pair."

What had happened to reduce the good intentions of two understanding single people to such animal-like actions? I couldn't even imagine the words coming out of Barbara's mouth, much less her spiteful actions.

Although I am always a little shocked when I or someone else does something startling, I am never really surprised. I learned a long time ago that almost everyone means well when they initiate a relationship, but unfortunately, *meaning well is not enough*! You see, satisfying relationships don't just happen. They are made. Very few people know how to make them, but because we have such needs and because most of us mean well, we keep trying.

When I talk to older people, they often communicate how much they've *tried* to build good relationships. Sadly, they say they just "happened" to run into all the wrong people. And all their good intentions never produced one lasting, intimate relationship.

Without God's perspective, human relationships inevitably self-destruct. In counseling singles, I have realized that it is important not only to share the biblical dimensions of relationships based on a faith commitment but to see why these relationships fail. The purpose of this chapter is to do just that.

There are no doubt many specific reasons why relationships fail, but I would like to share five general causes. (They fail, I might add, in spite of the best and most sincere attitude on the part of both partners.) Let us continue the story of Barbara and Kathy to see if we can understand why their good intentions were not enough.

Reason #1: Differing Backgrounds

In startling contrast to only fifty years ago, America has become a social melting pot. The travel explosion, increased job mobility, easier methods of communication, industrial growth, and television have resulted in people from all walks of life being exposed to each other. Today, your friends may have an entirely different background from yours. Widely diverse social values, religious activities, sports activities, political beliefs, financial practices, and personal habits are thrown together when two people meet. When they decide to share an apartment, that melting pot can turn into a pressure cooker overnight. Barbara and Kathy are good examples.

Barbara came from a very disciplined home. Kathy, on the other hand, came from a home established by outgoing parents who always seemed to be on the run. The very first day Barbara and Kathy spent together revealed these different backgrounds.

Barbara, a spotless housekeeper, observed the following things on the first morning after Kathy left for work: crumbs and a butter dish on the counter, an open cereal box on the table, and, from the evening before, a smudged glass half full of Coke on a dirty coffee table. Barbara's frustration intensified when she led the apartment maintenance man to the bathroom to fix a faucet. Dirty stockings and underclothes were strewn all over the tile floor. Barbara was upset. Imagine being identified with such a slob!

Kathy, herself, had left that morning fuming. The night before, Barbara, who goes to work later in the morning than Kathy, had watched TV until midnight. Then she decided to take a shower and wash her hair. The shower sounded like Niagara Falls to Kathy. Worst of all, Kathy had to get up and turn the hall light out twice because it was shining under her door after ten o'clock!

During that first week, even though they were both upset and had a few sharp words for each other, Kathy and Barbara quickly talked about their problems and said they were sorry. The following weekend, however, was frightening.

Saturday was not one of Barb's better days. She forgot to tell Kathy that "Mr. Wonderful" had called *twice*, which caused Kathy to miss a date. Later, Barb picked the wrong time to vacuum—during Kathy's "famous" Saturday afternoon nap.

Kathy was not at her best, either. While she was

preparing for a pool party she could not find a proper container for lemonade, so she asked to borrow Barbara's pitcher (an antique of her great grandmother's). Unfortunately, at the party the pitcher was hit by a volleyball and broken. Barb's patience ran out when the apartment manager called to tell her that the rent check had bounced. Kathy's reimbursement to her had been the cause of the problem.

In only a week, the girls' mutual respect for each other was severely tested. They began to see each other with totally new eyes. Tragically, their perceptions of each other did not improve over the next six months.

Barbara's budget was very tight, while Kathy never really knew how much money she had. Kathy had strong feelings about ERA and politics. Barbara inadvertently provoked her on both subjects. Barbara loved to read. Kathy liked the outdoors. She wanted their apartment to be the center of activity, but to Barbara, home was an escape from noise and excitement. The list seemed endless.

These two people meant so well, but in just a few short days, they found out they were very different. Obviously some of the conflicts resulted from sinful actions, but for the most part none of the conflicts necessarily demonstrated whose way of life was right or wrong. Yet, their differences in background certainly led to disagreement, even though they had meant so well in the beginning.

Barbara and Kathy's experience typify so many relationships between singles or marrieds. Two people expect to be compatible, but then they find out quickly that they approach life very differently. These differences lead to disagreements. Conflict results in hurt feelings, and hurt feelings cause the initial emotional attraction to falter. Of course, the sins of each person further color the picture. Finally, the natural motivation that brought the two people together is gone. What happens next will either make or break the relationship.

Reason #2: "You Do Your Part, I'll Do Mine"

When a relationship such as Barbara and Kathy's encounters the reality of their many differences, and the partners begin to lose their feelings of natural attraction, an underlying problem presents itself. They do not have a real understanding of how to maintain a relationship in light of their differences, strengths, and weaknesses.

Unfortunately, they often rely on a plan I call the "50-50 relationship," a plan we have all been taught by our cultural backgrounds. It works (or doesn't work!) something like this.

Sunday, following their big explosion on Saturday, Barbara and Kathy had a good talk. They were hurt, and most of the positive feelings they had for one another were gone. Yet they knew moving out after one week together was not only impractical but childish. They made an uneasy truce and decided to draw up a compromise.

Diligently, they worked out a contract to help correct each area of conflict. Optimistically, they agreed: You do your part, and I'll do mine. They began to feel better. Somehow this seemed right. After all, what could be wrong with a "team" approach? It sounded so good.

What Barbara and Kathy could not see was, the 50-50 relationship is inherently impossible. Why? Analyze it with me.

The success of the 50-50 relationship depends on the premise that the other person will meet you halfway. But knowing where the halfway point is is impossible. Why? You can neither live inside the other person's emotions nor possess precisely the same standards for "performance."

At the end of their "Saturday Night at the Fights" Barbara had run into her room and had cried for an hour, and Kathy had left, slamming the door, to take a long walk. Neither could be sure the one suffered—or cared—as much as the other did. Kathy couldn't cry Barbara's tears, and Barbara couldn't feel the tightness in the pit of Kathy's stomach. Neither could be sure the other was meeting halfway.

What happens in the 50-50 relationship is, both parties develop deeper and deeper disappointment in the other person. Each person is watching the other constantly, waiting for a chink in the commitment. The relationship becomes suffocating and performance-based. The list of "tests" grows at an increasing pace. Each person becomes more convinced that the other is not keeping up his or her part of the bargain.

Entering a single relationship naively by planning to meet your friend halfway guarantees the same results that Barbara and Kathy experienced. Christian and non-Christian alike end up in bitter frustration if they expect another human being to meet them at the proverbial pass. The 50-50 relationship is not an option if you're looking for happiness in human love.

Reason #3: Our Fallen Nature

So you've pursued a 50-50 relationship with your friend. Despite all honest and good intentions, the conflict intensifies to the point of explosion. Abruptly, you step back and are horrified to see that you are feeling love and concern for your friend one minute and hatred the next.

Why can't this negative process be stopped?

The Bible reveals that each of us is selfish, with a capacity for strong destructive actions. Failure to anticipate this tendency, understand it, and obey God's solution to it is the third major cause of relationship failure.

Singles who make commitments without knowing how to control this selfishness will soon devastate one another. Barbara, for example, is normally a very nice person. But in one of her disagreements with Kathy, she refused to speak to her roommate for several days. Kathy, enraged, purposely "forgot" to tell Barbara that her boss had called about a change in the work schedule, which meant Barb reported for her nursing shift twenty-four hours early!

A tense relationship, especially a living situation, where neither person feels secure, is fertile ground for all kinds of extreme behavior. Some people yell at one another, as Barbara and Kathy often did. Others use the silent treatment, refusing to be civil until their friend "shapes up." Redirecting a relationship in a performance-oriented environment is most difficult. Resentment and hurt from past arguments are so heavy in the air that it is almost impossible to get creative actions going again. Each person begins to really be fearful of the other, based on past performance. They imagine the worst and say, "Help! I'm trapped with a crazy monster!" Soon, all respect is lost. The pain and shock of seeing that sinful nature is so severe that singles "divorce," or run from their problems, as surely as many marrieds do.

Failure to anticipate the self-centered nature of yourself or a partner in a relationship is a costly mistake. Romans 3:10–18 describes the terrible potential of the self-centered nature when it is out of control. Ultimately, it can destroy any relationship.

Reason #4: Inability to Cope With Trials

Time and time again when roommates come in for counseling, one or both of them are going through a period of testing or trials that originally had no connection whatever to their relationship. Because of their failure to recognize and understand God's perspective on life, they attribute their stress to the closest target— their friend. This, of course, results in loss of trust and develops tendencies to judge one another instead of supporting each other.

Two men who were roommates came to see me. They were about to end a fine relationship. After several years of consistently good experiences, they had really struggled in the last seven months. As I began to ask questions, the following facts surfaced.

Over the last several months Erik's fiancé had begun to have doubts about their planned marriage. The doubts were not serious enough to break the engagement, but they were serious enough to cause daily anxiety for Erik. His self-image had suffered greatly.

On the other hand, Jerry, Erik's roommate, after four years as a service representative for a large corporation had been switched to sales representative. Sales goals really threatened Jerry. He was ten percent behind on his quota and was burdened by that problem almost constantly.

Both of these men were going through the normal trials of life; yet neither had properly recognized this fact in himself or communicated it to the other. Since their self-worth and future security were momentarily in jeopardy, both men were very volatile in their dealings with each other. Without realizing it, Erik and Jerry were venting frustrations due to outside problems on each other. Jerry and Erik initially were not having problems with each other, but with normal trials of life. But soon the pressures brought on by the trials were being blamed on the relationship.

Trials in life are not optional. People must learn to deal with them openly and keep them from destroying their relationships with others. If properly recognized for what they are (momentary maturing processes), trials can become rich blessings to a relationship.

Many people come into my office thinking that their friend has faltered, instead of realizing their friend's need to be supported. The problems are tremendous at times—dating, moving, changing jobs. Yet, seen in the light of wisdom, the pain of these problems can open the door to compassion, intimacy, and deeper commitment. Without that godly perspective, we will suffer psychological hangovers that can last a lifetime.

Expect your friend to experience ups and downs. After all, you do. Be sensitive enough to realize when something is bothering him or her. Support each other instead of criticizing and judging one another, thereby causing needless stress and hurt.

Reason #5: The Fantasy of Feelings

Life in America today is focused on the "pleasure" principle. If it feels good, do it. If it doesn't, run the other way! Before the 1960s, Americans focused on surviving and working for their share of the proverbial pie. Since then, shorter and shorter working hours, wealth, leisure time, worship of the body, the Great Society, and the human rights movement have caused all of us to focus more on *our* pleasure and rights. Certainly, there has been a lot of good in some of this change. But the negative effects have been devastating. People in general have lost their "sticking power"—to jobs, to obligations, and especially to relationships. People today are saying, "If it doesn't feel good, buddy, I am getting out!"

People—especially singles—must wake up and realize that they talk about love as if it were a mystic cloud that floats in and out of a relationship. Reminiscing regretfully is all too easy: "I remember when we first worked together on that summer project. Boy, I had such respect for her *then*." This initial rush of attraction and respect falters quickly when the relationship encounters problems.

Because all of us tend to be overly dependent on our emotions, love becomes ninety-nine percent feelings. Unfortunately, when life gets tough, if there is no solid commitment beneath those feelings, the "love" and "respect" evaporate like a vapor.

Much of our feelings in America today are predicated on fantasy. Marriages are being consummated, partnerships declared, and roommates established based on nothing more than emotional attraction. We need to get away from fantasy and into godly faith as the basis of relationships. Emotional attraction can change overnight by a reversal of circumstances: rich to poor, young to old, social to unsocial, athletic to unathletic, healthy to sick, and skinny to fat.

Failure to understand the commitment of real love is the major reason relationships fail. *All relationships that are based only on feelings, whether real or imagined, are simply counterfeit ways of trying to meet our needs.* God's love—perfect love—provides the only solid base for consistent feelings. Only through Him are lasting relationships possible. Only He can cover the faults and weaknesses of people like you and me and our friends.

7

Faith Relationships:
An Illustration from Marriage

"Okay, so I need to develop relationships . . . great!
The problem is, I've been trying for years without a lot to
show for it."

Comments like these are heard constantly in counseling rooms across America. All of us say we are open to
relationships, but few of us succeed.

Unfortunately, most of us approach relationships as if
we were writing a business contract. "If you will do this,
then I will do that. I will throw in this concession if you
will throw in that one." Most people approach new
relationships with the hope of writing a better contract.
Therefore, relationships are subconsciously computed
as a challenge to find someone who will enter into a fair
agreement with us. Our rights quickly become the overwhelming factor in such transactions.

The fact that God created us to relate to others matters
very little if we do not know *how* to establish successful
relationships. God's concept of faith relationships offers
the best way.

Faith Relationships

We have learned how God saw our need and established His purposes for relationships. But God didn't
stop there. He has given us the knowledge and insight to

release His people—and notably singles—to be successful in relationships. Apart from accepting Christ as my
Savior, no single truth has affected my own life more
than what God says in Genesis 1 and 2. These thoughts
have also revolutionized the lives of every person I know
who has understood and applied them.

God constructed human beings in such a way that we
must depend on Him before success is attainable in
relationships. God did this both to protect us from Satan
and to help us experience more out of life by learning to
trust Him first. Because there is no life, no lasting peace,
no true satisfaction apart from God, He graciously is
teaching us to depend utterly on Him.

God designed the perfect relationship when He
created Adam and Eve. Now, as a single, you may feel
slightly uncomfortable at this point, looking at a marriage illustration. But the spiritual principles here are
crucial to every relationship God has for us, whether it be
with friends of the same sex, friends of the opposite sex,
roommates, prayer partners, or a spouse.

In Genesis 2, God established the *faith relationship*.
Without question, Adam and Eve submitted to God's
plan, and the results were dynamic. The same steps to a
godly relationship are operative today for you. Consider
these five steps:

1) Admit your need for relationships.
2) Trust God for your relational needs.
3) Be willing to sacrifice for your need.
4) Receive God's provision for your need.
5) Receive God's blessing.

Step One: Admit Your Need

In the beginning, Adam was a perfect creation. His
environment was perfect, he had not sinned, and most

importantly, his relationship with God was perfect. Scripture says God and Adam walked and talked together. Adam actually experienced God with at least two of his physical senses. Even Christ Himself was later referred to as the "second Adam" because Christ was perfectly sinless as Adam originally was.

Me Plus God—Do I Need More?

> But God said, "It is not good for the man to be alone; I will make him a helper suitable for him" (Gen. 2:18).

Everything God had created prior to Adam was declared good, with no additions necessary. Adam could have developed the first inferiority complex when God said being alone was not good, if God had not explained.

Adam as a physical specimen was good, but he was "alone"—he was not yet finished. On the surface this conflicts with much of our past teaching from church and Bible studies. All we need is God! If all Adam needed was God, how could God say Adam was alone?

Listen well, singles! God is establishing without question that He created men and women to be incomplete without human relationships. God could have created humankind differently, but He chose to require individuals to need one another. So God tells Adam that He will make a helper suitable for him. His being alone was "not good." God was not yet finished with His creation. Adam and Eve are two parts of one creation from God's view. (In the same way, God views the church as one new creation made of several members: Christ's Bride.) These are mysteries that do not make sense humanly, but require faith.

Further Instruction

One would expect that God, after telling Adam He

was not yet complete, would then create Eve. Instead, God did something else.

> And out of the ground the LORD God formed every beast of the field and every bird of the sky, and brought them to the man to see what he would call them; and whatever the man called a living creature, that was its name. And the man gave names to all the cattle, and to the birds of the sky, and to every beast of the field, but for Adam there was not found a helper suitable for him (Gen. 2:19,20).

Why do you think God created the animals and had Adam name them before He created Eve? Object lesson number one from this passage is, as Dr. Howard Hendricks would say, "God never gives us anything without first showing us our need." Adam discovered his need called "aloneness" by naming the animals. ". . . but for Adam there was not found a helper suitable for him" (v. 20). Had God given Eve before Adam realized his need, he never would have fully appreciated her. God went out of His way to demonstrate the plan and pattern of His creation.

Thinking through how Adam must have discovered his need as he named the animals is entertaining, but our situation today is decidedly similar. We must first come to see our own God-given need for relationships before we can accept God's plan.

Step Two: Trust God for Your Relational Needs

After taking time out to show Adam his need for relationships, God created Eve.

> So the LORD God caused a deep sleep to fall upon the man, and he slept; then He took one of his ribs, and

closed up the flesh at that place. And the LORD God fashioned into a woman the rib which He had taken from the man, and brought her to the man (Gen. 2:21).

Scripture is so exciting in its detail! Adam's ability to sleep, induced by God, is a picture of total trust that God is in control. Adam trusted God, and "God brought Eve to Adam." But think about that for a minute. If Eve was created next to Adam, why was it necessary for God to bring her to Adam? I think God wanted to make sure Adam had no question about who had met his "aloneness" need. God wants us to know that *He personally and uniquely meets our most intimate needs for relationships.*

Can you believe that? In spite of your fears, your isolation, your desperate needs, can you *believe*? God created the need in us for others, but God's purpose is to cause us to trust in Him. In the last analysis, *God* was Adam's hope, not Eve. Yet God uses people, and people therefore are not optional.

Step Three: Be Willing to Sacrifice for Your Need

Because of the perfect state of Adam before the Fall, one may feel that Adam was not required to experience sacrifice for his relationship with Eve. Yet Adam was required to give up a rib to God before Eve was made, a symbol, among other things, of the humility and submission to God we should bring to every relationship. As small as Adam's sacrifice was, it was a forerunner of things to come. Sacrifice is vital in demonstrating commitment and in releasing a loving response in another person. Christ loved us, but until He died for us, we were not constrained to love Him in return. The sacrifice was, in fact, an investment that paid tremendous dividends. In the long run, Christ's sacrifice was turned to blessing because He saved His church.

Sacrifice is a necessary part of building faith relationships. Because God is involved, though, there ultimately is no loss, only gain.

Step Four: Receive God's Provision

Step four in faith relationships is life changing: our response to God's provision. When God brought Eve to Adam, Adam responded overwhelmingly.

> And the man said,
> "This is now bone of my bones,
> And flesh of my flesh;
> She shall be called Woman,
> Because she was taken out of Man" (Gen. 2:23).

Adam was excited! This translation of the Hebrew does not do Adam's response justice. Adam was getting up out of his chair, so to speak, shouting, "Hey, come over here!" There was no question; Eve was perfect for him.

What was the basis for Adam's total acceptance of Eve? Was it the fact that Adam had inspected lots of Eves and just picked one out? Certainly not. Adam had never seen another person, to say nothing of an Eve. Don't misunderstand. I'm sure Eve was attractive to him. But Adam's one hundred percent acceptance was not based on his inspection of her.

Adam's total acceptance was based on *who God was to him*. You see, God had created Adam. God had created his perfect environment. God had told him he was alone. God had created Eve. God had exhibited a faithful track record. Adam received Eve based not on human inspection, but on the certainty and trustworthiness of God.

Every relationship is established on some basis for success. Usually that basis is inspection of performance, which leads to destructive competition. Adam based his relationship on God's role as both author and guarantor of the relationship. Therefore, Adam trusted God and His promises—not Eve's performance. Singles must determine which friends God has placed next to them and then accept them based on God's faithfulness, in spite of those persons' weaknesses.

Step Five: Receive God's Blessing

Verses 24 and 25 of Genesis 2 summarize everything God did for Adam and Eve, and include an exciting promise:

> For this cause a man shall leave his father and his mother, and shall cleave to his wife; and they shall become one flesh. And the man and his wife were both naked and were not ashamed.

The passage focuses on the marriage relationship specifically, but the principle applies integrally to all our human relationships.

"... *a man shall leave his father and his mother.* ..." Before a significant relationship can form properly, there must be total devotion and commitment. The word "leave" means to abandon or break absolutely. God tells us that in marriage, both the man and woman must leave the authority of the old (their parents) before the new (their marriage) can stand firm. In the same way we as Christians must break our ties with the world before we commit ourselves to Christ and the church.

". . . *and shall cleave to his wife.* . . ." The word "cleave" is even stronger than "stick like glue." It describes how two materials are melted into one to produce a stronger substance, and the verb is used passively, meaning that the unifying work is accomplished by God. As in marriage, when God places us with another Christian friend, our ability to cleave to that friend as Adam cleaved to Eve will be determined by our faith. Will we believe, as Adam did, that God placed us together and that He will insure the outcome of the relationship? To the extent we believe God we will be free to be faithful friends, in spite of weakness. God will mold you together in a strong union.

". . . *and they shall become one flesh.* . . ." This passage has always been used to connote physical oneness in marriage, but oneness outside of marriage is referred to as oneness in Christ's Body, the church (see Eph. 4). When a person commits by faith to the new relationships God has provided, He promises unity.

The principle is absolute. Commitment based on the certainty of God's role in establishing relationships is vital. The only way any single will experience spiritual and emotional oneness with another person is by allowing God to join them by faith.

"And the man and his wife were both naked and were not ashamed." There are few promises of God that excite me more than this one. It is directed to married people, but the underlying principle is equally true for any faith relationship.

The meaning of this word "unashamed" is "total openness without fear of rejection." The physical implications for marriage are obvious, but God is speaking of the total person—intellectually and emotionally. In a faith relationship we are freed to be completely honest, transparent, and vulnerable to the other person—as they are freed to be honest, transparent, and vulnerable to us. How is this possible? Adam based his acceptance of Eve, not on her performance, but on God's faithfulness. And so must we when we enter a relationship.

It *is* possible to accept another person, whether as another single or as a married person, based on the same certainties that Adam had. I believe that as surely as God gave Eve to Adam, God gave me Sally. The transparency and freedom I share with her is proof of my initial faith. Sally and I have experienced similar faith relationships with other couples and singles whom God has given to support us. They are absolutely vital to us.

So you've been trying to establish meaningful relationships. But have you done it God's way? From the opening of Genesis, God demonstrates how He has a perfect order and purpose for relationships. And the first example He gave us of His plan was Adam and Eve, the first relationship here on earth.

We need God. Ultimately only He can fulfill our needs. But He gave us others with a purpose in mind. And as we seek Him to supply our relationships, He will provide abundantly.

8

Faith Relationships:
An Illustration from Jonathan and David

"I am so afraid you're going to convince me to stay single! I know I should trust God, but I want so much to get married."

These words have come from the mouth of almost every single I know. And how many of us know the feeling. It is like the man who brought his son to Jesus to be healed. "I do believe," he cried, "help my unbelief" (Mark 9:24).

Perhaps you nodded your head as you read about relationships in the previous chapter. But now, you must get up in the morning, go back to work, and deal with the fact all over again that you are still *single*.

Don't shut God out at this point. Over ninety percent of Americans get married without God's help. If God truly wills for you to get married, be sure: It will happen! But God calls you to learn to trust Him *today* in faith relationships, so He can protect and bless you if and when marriage does come. And remember: Marriage was never designed to fulfill *all* your relational needs. Relationships established today are resources through which God will meet your needs even after marriage.

The fear of staying single is, in actuality, a fear of being alone. Unfortunately, our culture has taught us that only marriage will fulfill the emotional fantasies of our mind.

This completely contradicts all of God's good (and they are good) purposes. God established a dual structure in which to meet our "aloneness" needs.

The Church and Relationships

The counterpart to marriage in God's structure is the church. In God's strategy, believers should consider their role in the Body of Christ as absolute as they consider marriage. But tragically, nothing could be further from the way the situation is for most Christians.

Church is rarely thought of in such glowing terms as marriage. Yet, in *God's* mind the church allows singles to be completed—even by the opposite sex in the proper sense—so that they reflect God's image, reproduce godly disciples, and rule the earth for God. How sad that the church generally is not functioning well for and with singles. Singles should be a vital part of the cutting edge of God's church. Paul clearly gives this impression in 1 Corinthians 7, as we have noted in Part I.

Isolated, fearful singles should be finding their security in God's church. But how often is that the case? When I mention the word *church*, for example, what comes to mind? A building, a denomination, a particular pastor, or a particular type of service? None of these things capture what God has in mind. In Scripture the word *church* is the Greek word *ekklesia*, which means "called out." God's church is not a building or denomination, but people who have been called out of the world by accepting Christ and are being built up together. The church is people who have a common bond in Christ.

The apostle Paul spoke to the Ephesians about God's church. He mentions the security that the church is to provide.

> So then you are no longer strangers and aliens, but you are fellow citizens with the saints, and are of God's household, having been built upon the foundation of the apostles and prophets, Christ Jesus Himself being the corner stone, in whom the whole building, being fitted together is growing into a holy temple in the Lord; in whom you also are being built together into a dwelling of God in the Spirit (Eph. 2:19–22).

Most singles who are fearful of missing out on marriage feel like a stranger and alien in our culture. But Paul says we are fellow citizens in God's household or church.

Christ Himself is the Head of this church, and He is fitting each person into the whole as the church grows into the holy temple of Christ. The result is one Body, made up by many members, unified by God's Holy Spirit. From God's point of view, this relationship is as emphatic as marriage itself. Singles should be firmly implanted in God's functioning Body.

An Example of a Single Relationship

The church is the place where singles should first establish relationships. Within that context, relationships contain the same five dimensions that the marriage relationship does. An excellent example of such a relationship is Jonathan and David's in the Old Testament.

Jonathan, the eldest son of King Saul, listened to God and loved David with the same faith with which Adam loved Eve. Even though Jonathan, humanly speaking, was the rightful heir to the throne, he forfeited that right to allow David to become king, completing God's will for the nation Israel. The passage we will look at here describes the sequence of events after David killed the

giant and saved Israel for Saul. Observe the five steps to
the faith relationship again, this time as enacted between
two godly singles.

Jonathan Admitted His Need and God Provided

After the giant was killed, (see 1 Samuel 17), Jonathan
opened his heart to David:

Now it came about when he had finished speaking to
Saul, that the soul of Jonathan was knit to the soul of
David, and Jonathan loved him as himself (1 Sam. 18:1).

Every faith relationship—even casual friendships—
start by admitting one's need. And no person should
allow his or her soul to be knit to another without seeking
God to fulfill that need. Jonathan released himself to
God, and God provided David.

Proverbs 4:23 says, "Watch over your heart with all
diligence,/For from it flow the issues of life." God provided for Jonathan the very relationship He knew
Jonathan needed at the time. Only the friendship with
David, another man, could meet certain needs for
Jonathan. For Jonathan to rely on his own judgment for a
relationship would have been disastrous.

Jonathan Sacrificed for David

In response to God's provision, Jonathan obeyed the
command to "love thy neighbor as thyself." Verse 3 says:

Then Jonathan made a covenant with David because he
loved him as himself.

Jonathan demonstrated his acceptance of David by
verbalizing a strong commitment to his friend. The word

covenant is the same Hebrew word that is used in describing God's covenant with mankind: an everlasting commitment. But Jonathan also followed his words with action.

The name *Jonathan* translated in Hebrew means "the Lord gives," and Jonathan fulfills his name in verse 4:

> And Jonathan stripped himself of the robe that was on him and gave it to David, with his armor, including his sword and his bow and his belt.

Jonathan *sacrificed* for David. Knowing well the significance of his acts, he gave David his most prized possession, his battle regalia. The gift reflected Jonathan's personal accomplishments, his right to the throne—everything that he was and had as a person. David, and those around him, knew then that Jonathan's commitment was not taken lightly.

Jonathan continued to sacrifice for David. First Samuel 19 tells how Saul became jealous of David and tried to kill him. Jonathan saved David's life by talking Saul out of killing David. Jonathan went to bat for David! He sacrificed for him in every way possible. He spoke well of David, gave of his time and his possessions, and ultimately sacrificed his own place in life for him.

Jonathan Received a Blessing

After months of sacrificial action on Jonathan's part, God proved the value of faith by moving in David's heart.

> . . . David rose from the south side and fell on his face to the ground, and bowed three times. And they kissed each other [Jewish custom], and wept together, but David more (1 Sam. 20:42).

Up until this moment, every act of love in this relationship was initiated by Jonathan. Finally Jonathan's faith
overwhelmed David. David came out after Jonathan
saved his life a second time, and fell on the ground, and
bowed to Jonathan three times. They wept with joy for
one another, but David wept more. The Hebrew word
used means "exceedingly more." In other words, David
responded to Jonathan overwhelmingly. Jonathan's
faithfulness paid off.

Jonathan's Hope Was in God's Faithfulness

After David's expression of love and gratitude,
Jonathan revealed the basis of his ability to be faithful in a
seemingly one-sided relationship.

> And Jonathan said to David, "Go in safety, inasmuch as
> we have sworn to each other in the name of the LORD,
> saying, "The LORD will be between me and you, and
> between my descendants and your descendants for-
> ever". . . (1 Sam. 20:42).

The key phrase here is, "The Lord will be between me
and you . . . forever." Unequivocally, Jonathan saw
God as the hope of his relationship with David. Had
Jonathan looked at human circumstances—his father's
hatred, the "give-give-give" on his part—he would have
never been able to persevere. Instead, Jonathan had a
faith perspective. He knew God's faithfulness, and he
knew God was the author of his relationship with David.

The Faith Relationship and You

Single, if no one ever weeps "exceedingly more" for
you, if you never speak of commitment as Jonathan did,

you will have missed much of what life is about. It will never happen until *you* become a Jonathan and apply these five steps in a faith relationship with someone.

There is so much talk about self-image today. Look sharp, be sharp, and be cool. The world calls us to compete. But God calls us to serve—to lay our lives down for those people with whom He places us in relationships. Singles, God has a plan. You *need* Jonathan and David relationships.

Several months after hearing a similar talk, a single challenged me with this, "You really frustrated me several months ago by getting my hopes up. I've looked all over for someone to relate to but I can't find anyone." Listen, there are lots of Davids out there, but very few Jonathans. If you're looking for a Jonathan, good luck. If you are planning on becoming a Jonathan, you will have no problem finding countless Davids—and God's blessing.

When Jonathan was killed in battle, a grieving King David described Jonathan's impact on him eloquently.

> ". . . my brother Jonathan;
> You have been very pleasant to me.
> Your love to me was more wonderful
> Than the love of women" (2 Sam. 1:26).

We all know the sins David committed as a result of his uncontrollable attraction to women. Jonathan's godly love and friendship met needs in this "man's man" the opposite sex had not been able to.

The only reason to get married is if God plans it. God will meet your need for relationships as you seek His way and begin to trust Him. And God has His own family to draw from—just for you.

9

I'll Take That One

"I've got a thousand questions," a concerned single responded after a series of lectures. "If God is placing people around me to meet my needs, how do I recognize them? And how many people can I possibly love by faith like Jonathan did David? If there are too many, I won't have time to work."

I am aware how tough it is to establish relationships. In no other area does discouragement occur so easily.

Relax! The first step comes in realizing that God has not put the burden of looking for relationships on you. Placing people in your path is God's role. Your responsibility, single, is simply to be abiding in Him so that you will recognize God's relationships for you. In no way does God want you to start putting ads in the "Personals" columns, frequenting social clubs, or organizing a major campaign to establish five meaningful relationships in six months. God is a God of natural order and of peace.

What God wants for each of us is an environment of godly relationships which He will use to meet our needs (and He, in turn, will use us to meet others' needs). This environment should have a spectrum of relationships—some more intimate than others, but all submitted to Him so that He can use them as He wills without resistance from us.

All of us pass people on the street, in the grocery store, on the highway, every day. In one sense, we have no relationship with these people unless an outside action happens—you dent someone else's fender, a child smiles and you enjoy his sweetness with another on-looker, you stand in line together waiting to pay a bill for half an hour. These "relationships" are on the outer fringes of our lives.

Then there are those we know only to say hello to—people at work, neighbors, the mailman, the lady you ride the bus with. These acquaintances may or may not develop into relationships, as you spend time together or share common bonds. Often people at church are in this category; some become more intimate than others.

Most people have these say-hello-to type friends, and the next higher level—"good friends." But at the core of any single's life there should be at least one relationship modeled after Jonathan and David's: totally supportive, sacrificial, and based on a lasting faith acceptance. Then, ideally, each single should have several other relation-ships with a lesser, but still high, commitment level. Such commitments can even be to married couples, although such relationships may be more difficult to define. This environment provides a framework of committed individuals through which God will meet highly personal needs. We need all four levels of rela-tionships: concern, corporate, commitment, and cove-nant. Let's look at how God intended for us to relate to other people.

Concern Relationships

Scripture clearly depicts that we are to have a concern

for all people in general. Concern relationships are very general in the sense that we are equally aware and committed to all people. This type of relationship is tested only occasionally by some incident. For example, we may help a person with a flat tire on the side of the highway. Biblically, we have an example in the Good Samaritan (see Luke 10:30–37).

These relationships do not demand much of us, but we need that level of interaction with the world.

Corporate Relationships

Corporate relationships are those that involve specific placement in a group of people. When you become a member of a church, business corporation, Bible study, or club, you have a "built-in" relationship with each one in the group. If I discover that a person I work with goes to my church, we experience a kindred feeling and perhaps develop the relationship further. As you come to see that another person has been placed with you in a corporate group, your responsibility toward that person becomes increasingly more defined. It is time to begin considering God's purpose for that relationship.

God does not expect you to establish Jonathan-David relationships with lots of people. However, even in a group, you need to be sensitive to His leading. Would He have you just be friendly and say an encouraging word? Or should you spend time with this person?

Obviously, if two or three hundred members are involved, this corporate level of relationship will be very general in nature. But you can be specific in your application of sacrificial love to individuals. God would have us always looking out for those He would bring to us.

Commitment Relationships

Anytime God places a person in a close and consistently vulnerable relationship with you, your responsibility to apply aspects of faith commitment is increased.

Usually that close relationship arises out of a corporate relationship—someone who goes to the same church or Bible study group as you do or who is in the same club or department at work.

The faith *commitment* level of relationships is enacted at the point when God's command to love thy neighbor as thyself finally begins to have specific names and faces attached to it. In the same way as in marriage, you begin responding to the evidence that God has specifically placed these people next to you. Therefore, respond by receiving them from God by faith. Based on Scripture, make a commitment to them (verbal and demonstrative) that is strong enough to meet their needs under the pressure of the circumstances involved. Commitment relationships for one person may involve ten to fifteen people at any one time. Many times commitment relationships may be one-sided, if the receiving partner is not mature enough to understand biblical faith. However, a single's one-sided love can lead to exciting effects in the other person's life.

Consistent contact and vulnerability in a relationship demands God's perspective in order to avoid typical human problems. For example, in my church I am on the board of elders. Every member of that board previously chose to join our church, demonstrating evidence of God's leading us together. Among the church at large there are five of us who have been chosen to take on additional responsibility. This has given me further evidence of God's placing me with these particular men.

I see the corporate group of believers on Sunday, but the board of elders I see more regularly because of our mutual responsibilities. The responsibilities we share together are more complex and demand deeper involvement of our intimate selves. Therefore, our commitment and application of God's love and faith principles is of absolute importance, otherwise we might experience division and misunderstanding in the course of doing our duties as elders.

The example I have given is of mature men in the Lord. One needs to approach commitment level relationships carefully. We can be strong influences for good for Christians who are less mature than we are (as others will be for us), but God has warned us not to be unequally yoked to unbelievers—even in a deep friendship (see 2 Cor. 6:14). Adam and Eve and Jonathan and David were all people of God. God will not lead us into deep relationships that would weaken or draw us away from our commitment to Him.

Covenant Relationships

The last level of relationships is that of the Jonathan and David experience. This level is unique from the others. First, it is unique because it involves two mature Christians with a strong mutual commitment. The other levels may be mainly one-sided in commitment, but not with a covenant relationship. (Jonathan and David's relationship changed from commitment to covenant, when David finally responded.) The commitment is not based primarily on emotional attraction, but on mutual belief that God has placed them together for a purpose.

Let me give you an example. I first met Barry Leventhal in the spring of 1967. We worked for the same company and decided to share an apartment, too. From the very beginning of our relationship, we were significant in each other's life. Barry helped me greatly in my spiritual development that first year, and I was important to him in some practical ways. Several years later, after finishing graduate school, Barry joined me in starting Christian Family Life, a counseling service. After several years, God began to lead Barry into the pastorate, and I helped him find a place to start a church. Our mutual love and need for one another has kept our relationship vibrant these last fourteen years, despite the miles between us. Barry has just finished his doctorate and hopes to work with me again sometime in the future. Our commitment will continue for a lifetime.

Barry's and my commitment to each other goes beyond emotional attraction. Our responsibility to each other is based on the faith that God has given us each other for a purpose. Barry has been more than just a good friend. He has been absolutely essential to who I am and what I am doing today. *God* is between Barry and me.

I mention this example to demonstrate how specific God's evidence of two people being placed together can be. Because Barry also believes strongly that God has placed us together for a purpose, the honesty and supportiveness of our relationship is fantastic.

Relationships like these are few in number. One in your life is sufficient, two an absolute revolution, and if God has given you more, you are truly blessed!

Covenant relationships demonstrate their value during times of suffering more than at any other time. Peter wrote, "Beloved, do not be surprised at the fiery ordeal among you, which comes upon you for your testing, as though some strange thing were happening to you" (1 Pet. 4:12). People who are not prepared for trials and suffering can expect their suffering to be coupled with anxiety, fears, and depression. Expect trials, but be prepared by establishing strong relationships that can help support you. The community of believers is invaluable to you, especially during trials.

As you begin to think about these levels of relationships, it becomes clear that the turning point for a covenant relationship comes at the *commitment* level. Which people has God placed close enough to me, so that I have contact with them regularly without having to seek them out? Barry started out as a roommate and working partner, but over time, God developed much more.

Where do you look for covenant relationships? Primarily, one of three places: 1) your church or Bible study group, 2) job or regular recreational activities, 3) living situations.

When God naturally gives you regular time with another person, without special effort on your part, that can be evidence of a unique placement. Many times we take for granted those people right under our noses. If you begin to survey your working environment, church, neighborhood, social groups, and recreational groups, you will begin to sense possibilities. Again: The importance of this relationship being between two Christians cannot be overemphasized.

At this point, counsel from an older or more mature Christian will give you wisdom about how to approach the person. The more spiritually open the person is, the more freedom there will be to discuss relationship possibilities with him or her. In most cases, your consistent concern—through listening, being interested in the other person, and just being around—will communicate much more than words.

When the time comes to verbalize your commitment, share the biblical reasoning behind your action. Any two people can be emotionally attracted, but the uniqueness of your commitment is of faith. And faith is established by the Word of God.

In our culture of "macho" men and homosexuality, it is very unnatural to verbalize commitment to another person. Yet verbalizing commitment is absolutely necessary since words are the way humans communicate. What good is a commitment if the other person doesn't know about it? Could we understand God's love for us without the Scripture (words)? Certainly not.

There are four things to remember when verbalizing a commitment to a new friend:

1) Do not come on too strong initially with words such as "I love you."

2) Give the person a chance to respond to initial low-key statements before giving the whole perspective.

3) State clearly what you do *not* mean.

4) Use Scripture to explain what you do mean to insure the maturity of your intention.

Ingredients of a Successful Relationship

A single friend came up at the break in the afternoon session of the seminar where I was speaking. I could tell he was perplexed. "Okay," he said, "I think I know a friend that God has placed next to me for a relationship. My question is, 'How do you love a friend?' " What a great question! More people need to ask, because very few ever consider the ingredients necessary to a friendship.

I would like to suggest eight ingredients. These include attitudes and actions that each person involved should consider carefully. They are *faith, humility, servanthood, commitment, vulnerability, availability, encouragement,* and *prayer.* Each of these carries a certain cost factor. Evaluate your relationships to see if these qualities are present. The potential reward is great!

Faith

As we discussed earlier, the quality that distinguishes godly relationships from worldly relationships is faith. No longer is the relationship founded on our human performance. We are set free, because God is both the author and the guarantor of the relationship.

Faith means believing a statement or promise of God irrespective of human instinct. That principle takes us out of the animal realm and allows us to experience the alternative to human impulse.

The person who dares to believe that a friend is a provision of God, instead of a competitor or a threat, can care and give to the relationship without fear, because he or she knows God is in control. A person who is trusting God to meet his or her needs, in spite of a friend's momentary "bad" performance, is free to bless that person even though they may not humanly deserve it. Therefore, the relationship is spared, and the friend can be healed instead of damned.

Humility

Encouragement, love, fellowship, affection, and concern from others are what most people are looking for in relationships. Unfortunately, very few find their dreams.

The apostle Paul, in a letter to friends, stated that those who hope for these rewards cannot be selfish in relationships. Instead, each must have "humility of mind" and regard friends as "more important than himself" (Phil. 2:1–4).

Every serious relational problem I have ever tried to help resolve involved two competitive people who were fighting for their rights. Paul said that the fighting, self-centered instincts of humankind will never result in love and affection. Yet we can easily get so angry and competitive that we become blinded to even our own best interests. Often, retribution and retaliation seem to be the only human responses we understand. Typically, at the height of these conflicts, we all deeply resent the thought of considering our enemy as more important than ourselves.

The key phrase in Paul's statement is "humility of mind," with the emphasis on *mind*. Most people define humility as becoming a "doormat" or a "weakling" to other people. Meekness has become a dirty word in our culture, and granted, some Christians do become self-destructive. This concept of humility could not be further from the truth to which Paul was referring.

The humility Paul was speaking of results from knowing God's perspective concerning relationships. In fact, Paul illustrated the principle by describing Christ's mental attitude (see vv. 5–7). We should be free to consider our friends more important than ourselves because of what we know by faith. As Christ trusted in His heavenly Father's words, yet was willing to suffer, we also should be willing even to suffer, in order that our friends might be lifted up. The result in Christ's life was external exaltation. The same result is imputed to us and is experienced now in the form of returned encouragement, love, fellowship, affection, and concern from others.

But, you may ask, how is God able to bless me when

my friend has so many weaknesses? Is God the author
and guarantor of relationships or not? Believe me, retaliation doesn't work! God's way is humility based on His
trustworthiness.

Every faith relationship involves two people who are
free to give the other person preference over themselves.
Entering a relationship with this servant-like attitude
makes a significant difference in the quality and benefits
of any relationship.

Servanthood

Closely related to humility—and equally misunder-
stood—is the principle of servanthood in relationships.
"I am not going to do things for people who don't
appreciate me and even hurt me while I am doing them"
is our normal response to the idea of servanthood.
Giving to people without first getting is not logical,
humanly speaking. Servanthood sounds too much like
slavery. Remember: We are talking about a relationship
that is not intended to be typical. In a faith relationship,
the willingness to sacrifice for a friend is primary. Christ
said He came not to be served, but to serve others. He
went on to say, "If I then, the Lord and the Teacher,
washed your feet, you also ought to wash one another's
feet" (John 13:14). Are you willing to wash your friend's
feet?

In our feelings- and pleasure-oriented society, sacrifice is not popular. But sacrifice is a crucial ingredient in
God's plan of relationships.

Normally when a relationship demands sacrifice our
natural response is to insult the person. Servanthood is
the form of communication that stops the "insult cycle"
and sets the "appreciation cycle" in motion. If we serve
the person instead of insulting him, we establish a dif-

ferent dynamic. I am motivated when Sally says she loves me, but when she demonstrates her love sacrificially, responding is not just reasonable, I long to do so.

Commitment

The byword of most relationships is *fear*. John the apostle said this about fear and love: "There is no fear in love; but perfect love casts out fear . . . " (1 John 4:18). There is a direct correlation between fear in a relationship and the quality of love between the participants.

The most distinctive aspect about Christ's love toward man was that His love knew no limit. John 13:1 tells us that "He loved them to the end." Christ's love overcame every cost factor that would have caused Him to faint in His commitment. Even death could not keep Christ from His commitments.

A person who is faithful and consistent in a commitment to his or her friends is refreshingly unique. Commitments based on superficial feelings or selfish criteria are not worth the breath they're spoken with. Our insecurities and fears about relationships are largely the result of believing superficial statements we have heard before.

Consider the basis of your commitments. Are they just words or are they made based on faith that *God* will enable you to keep them?

Vulnerability

"Macho Man" is a song that made a hit with many Americans. The tune is catchy but the concept is devastating. Our society has placed so much emphasis on the macho image that few people have the freedom to communicate personal need. In our culture, to admit a personal concern or desperate need to another person is to communicate weakness.

In a faith relationship, admitting personal need opens the door to communication. Honesty concerning one's need is vital in releasing the same freedom in the other person.

The apostle Paul was "tough" enough to fit an American definition of masculinity; yet he said, " . . . we were burdened excessively, beyond our strength, so that we despaired even of life" (2 Cor. 1:8). Christ, the night before He died, said to His disciples, " 'My soul is deeply grieved, to the point of death; remain here and keep watch with Me' " (Matt. 26:38). If Paul and Christ admitted their needs and struggles, need we be afraid to admit our needs as well?

Overdependency or a failure complex is not the result of vulnerability in faith. Vulnerability is simple openness about the deep needs in one's life. Honest vulnerability is important because it says, "I need you, I trust you, I respect you, and I care about you."

Significant relationships are based on mutual caring and support. Many of us "macho" ourselves right out of relationships.

Availability

"Sure, I am committed to you," say many singles, "but on *my* terms and *my* timing." Faith relationships require sensitivity to a friend's needs, as the need occurs. Jonathan told David, " 'Whatever you say, I will do for you' " (1 Sam. 20:4). And he was faithful in his promise. Jonathan was open to serve David at all times, whether it was easy and convenient or not.

Probably the greatest evidence of the principle of

availability is caring enough to be a good listener. Many times, after counseling for several hours with someone, I know much more about their present needs than their friends of several years. Why? Because of the time I devoted to *listening*. Humility and servanthood are necessary to being a good listener. Listening with concern says "I love you" louder than words.

Other evidence of availability involves giving of one's time and resources. A single who is in touch with a friend's present needs and is available to meet those needs on the spot, with every resource at his or her command, is priceless.

Encouragement

"Sure, I think my friend is important and talented, but do I really have to tell him?" There is a mechanism operative, in men particularly, that blocks the ability to verbalize appreciation and encouragement. In the early stages of a friendship, encouragement is constantly on the tips of our tongues. However, if we do not verbalize our sentiments from the beginning, time can paralyze our tongues almost completely.

Add to that the fact that as a relationship develops over time, subtle competition also develops. If we are overly positive about a friend after that point, subconsciously we feel we are revealing inadequacies in ourselves.

Encouragement is essential to a relationship. An encouraging person is like a breath of fresh air! There is a special quality in a person who is selfless enough to be positive toward others. Paul exhorted, "And let us consider how to stimulate one another to love and good deeds . . . encouraging one another . . ." (Heb. 10:24,25). A single person can affect a friend's day positively by caring enough to be encouraging. Recognizing some quality or talent verbally or communicating solid confidence or belief in a friend can be life-changing.

Prayer

To the non-Christian and the nominal Christian, prayer is a redundant, merely religious act. But to the committed believer who is trying hard to develop relationships, prayer is a comforting refuge.

One need not be very perceptive to realize that relationships require significant self-sacrifice. True prayer is a direct line to the power and wisdom of the living God. Prayer is another primary way of seeing change in a friend (brought about by God, not you!) or expressing an honest hurt that needs venting. Prayer also serves to remind us of God's precious promises, which are the source of hope for men and women of faith.

10

The Dating Game

I have sometimes compared dating to buying a car.

In our teen years we try dates out like test driving. We check the acceleration, ask about gas mileage, and maybe kick the tires. Later, in our early twenties, we get a little fearful and decide to do without a few options. At twenty-five we panic and take whatever they have in stock. Then there are some buyers who finally realize they may never get a car at all. So they make do with an occasional joy ride, the thrill of sitting behind the wheel just for a while.

In a real sense, the whole American concept of dating is based upon deceiving one's self. Men with moral life-styles often are looking for women with the spirituality of their mom and the moves of Raquel Welch. Women, on the other hand, are looking for men who are a cross between St. Paul and Robert Redford. What is really scary is that more singles than I can believe think they have found a prince in shining armor or a promenade queen. Talk about being starry-eyed!

How does dating fit into the concept of faith relationships? Can a single Christian establish a relationship by means of dating? What are the pitfalls to beware?

The Rules of the Game

From the outset, I must be blunt: Dating as the world sees it is a faulty system of getting acquainted, but as a system of determining God's will for marriage, it is absolutely disastrous.

Reality in relationships is a must. Yet false impressions are the name of the dating game. I have seen appearances alter fifty percent between five o'clock work time and eight o'clock date time—and personality changes go for broke.

The charade continues as past facts are conveniently hidden and slight additions to reality are shared during the traditional "impress him/her session" of the first date. Anger, insecurity, and criticism are also carefully suppressed or camouflaged. Amazingly, all of this is done with little conscious intent to mislead. To a degree, the system makes you do it. It is a game we have *learned*. No wonder I run into person after person who, just months after marriage, says, "Who is this person I married?"

Even worse is the tremendous emphasis placed on performance in dating. The basis of the performance is external qualities, beginning with physical attractiveness. A certain scale of appearance is set up, and comments like "If I could just get her to jog, her thighs wouldn't be so big" are standard.

There is the perfect personality as well, and any deviations from that ideal are unacceptable. "He sounds like he honks when he laughs." "She is too assertive for me." "Everyone seems to like him, so of *course* I do, too!"

Perhaps the most dehumanizing checklist is for sexual attraction. After the first date the analysis is either "I find myself thinking of cold oatmeal when I kiss her" or "She really lights my fire!"

A certain kind of "spiritual macho" easily creeps into Christian relationships. "Well, you know he hasn't been to the 'Earnest Life Seminar' so I'm not sure he could be my spiritual leader," or "He's really on the ball spiritually." The list is endless.

All of these checklists emphasize the superficial realm and perpetuate the dating lie. The flaw of flaws in dating is the fact that feelings determine commitment. People decide to jump into bed together, alter careers, break spiritual commitments, or get married based solely on feelings of "I'll die if I lose you" or "It feels so good."

Don't get me wrong. High emotional feelings are of utmost importance in life. God created emotions, and He certainly desires that all people, singles included, experience emotion, not only toward other humans, but toward God Himself. However, from God's perspective, emotions are the *result* of a faith commitment, *not the basis* of the commitment.

How important this is to remember in dating. Feelings are fickle! A touch, a special situation, or partial enactment of a fantasy can create all kinds of feelings. However, the stark light of reality reveals the truth about those feelings. To base any major decision in life solely on feelings is suicidal. Yet the number one objective of dating is to discover how you feel about the other person.

Since dating is here to stay, at least in our society, and since God certainly expects single men and women to relate in some way, what can be done? The crucial truth for Christians in dating is to realize that *the purpose of godly dating is to determine His will in the relationship*. God

is a God of "yes's" and "no's," not gray zones. He either
intends a partnership or He doesn't.

Frankly, most singles, even Christians, are not willing
to yield to God's will. In their heart, they are afraid that
God will stick them with a dud. If they cannot trust God,
they must urgently trust themselves, and they end up
beaten by the system. Fantasy, performance, and feelings are the only recourse.

Singles, commit yourself to dating as a means of
determining God's will—and assume the answer to
progress in a relationship is "no" until He says "yes"
clearly. This is the first step in freeing yourself to look at
dating relationships honestly. But beware: There are
more pitfalls down the road.

Premature Communication

It's your first date with her. You're on the board of the
local singles outreach ministry; she is director of the
church choir. You both are spiritually mature, and you
find yourselves talking easily about your spiritual struggles and triumphs. Before you know it, you are both
asking in the back of your minds, "Say, are you serious
about anyone?" And the next thing you know, you've
opened your mouth to share your most intimate need of
the moment. Unfortunately, one of two things usually
occurs at this point. If your date is "available," and if she
also feels needful inside, she too will pour out the
burdens of her heart, intermingled with a long, detailed
history. Most likely, you will hold hands and kiss before
the date ends. And you'll both float home to tell your
roommates about your "unique" experience.

On the other hand, if one of you reacts to the "confession" by saying, "Hey, slow down," or with a disinterested "Hmmm . . . " a tremendous shock takes place. The vulnerable person now feels embarrassed and rejected. He or she has lost equal standing in the relationship. Dignity in tatters, the vulnerable single decides never to see that person again. With false bravado he says, "I'll show *her*," or she says, "Who needs *him*?"

I call such premature communication in dating *muddy water*. *Muddy water* is any kind of premature openness that causes negative anxiety in a dating relationship. And premature sexual communication (even a peck on the cheek) is a prime culprit. One or two launches into that water, and it's no wonder many Christian singles are fearful of dating.

A primary absolute principle of dating for every single is to never let muddy water negate the positive aspects of the dating relationship. Before couples realize it, the relationship is creating more emotional anxiety and pressure than joy and fun.

If muddy water and anxiety begin to build, stop the serious discussion and demands on one another. Reestablish the joy and fun of activities to the relationship. No matter what the outcome of the relationship, it is much easier to trust God with it if both parties follow through with self-control. God has all the time in the world to fill your needs, and He will not allow His mate for you get away. His role is seen much more clearly if the couple strives for a positive relationship.

Only God can meet your needs, as we have stated throughout this book. But our society continually conditions us to try to meet our needs by using other people—especially dating partners. When we have not allowed God to fulfill our needs for security, love, and acceptance, we are much more tempted to try to meet those needs by dating. Our anxiety is what pushes us into muddy water.

Be at peace in God's love. Trust that He will meet your needs for love, caring, affection, and security in His timing. Such a bedrock of trust frees you to see your current dating relationship as it is. It may be only a "fun" friendship. Accept it for that, and know God will meet your other needs through other people or through meaningful times with Him. Allow God to work freely; allow *Him* to develop your relationships, and rejoice in His gifts for this specific moment.

Gray Zones

The period which comes somewhere between a friendship and a solid commitment to marriage is one of the most difficult times in dating. I call this the "gray zone."

This time may seem "gray" to you—but it is never so to God. God's purposes in a relationship are always specific, concrete, and absolute, and we should never fool ourselves into thinking that God's will is hazy. God says "no" to the development of a relationship, until He knows it is time for "yes."

We all want to do what we want to do. There is something in all of us that hates absolutes, and we hate the absolute "no's" in dating for two reasons: They keep us from dabbling in sexual areas intended for marriage, and they keep the wrong relationships from developing into marriage (especially when we are desperate simply to get married).

The following guideline is an accurate way to evaluate this troubled state. You need to be asking: Where is the relationship going? Am I in God's will? I encourage singles to continue a friendship dating relationship as long as the following statements are true.

1. Neither person's spiritual life is negatively affected by the relationship. If a person's spiritual growth is being stunted and he or she has one foot in marriage, tragic consequences are just around the corner.

2. Neither person's life goals, such as job, friends, church, and recreational and artistic pursuits are being affected negatively by this relationship.

3. Neither party begins to participate in or depend on activities that God intends for marriage. Examples would be sexual involvement, inordinate emotional dependence, too much time together—all of which upset the balance of other commitments.

Creative Friendships

There must be a framework and purpose to any effective relationship. We quickly rebel against such analyses of our relationships, claiming that they kill "spontaneity," but God always gives us a structure—His will—in which to operate freely and to enjoy life truly.

I have been able to see real success with the following framework for dating relationships. Consider the order, freedom, and clarity these guidelines provide.

1. Determine to date only Christians—people who have put their trust in God and in Christ as their Savior and who are committed to a church that exalts Christ and teaches His Word.

2. Determine to be a creative friend, but let neither of you feel any obligation beyond friendship. Do not take

anything for granted—how you feel about each other, where the relationship is headed—no matter how much you might enjoy each other's company. Be sure that if nothing is communicated verbally, probably nothing is there.

3. Determine to be carefully but totally honest about your feelings, after testing them out first in prayer alone with God. Don't be afraid, but after prayer, tell your friend of any change you feel toward him or her.

4. Other than normal affectionate courtesies, make a firm commitment not to touch each other unless God is giving definite evidence of His calling you together toward marriage.

5. At such point that you both believe God is calling you to marriage, commit yourself to a specific time period in which to evaluate God's leading, to be confirmed by a mature godly Christian in your church or a Christian counselor. During this time, limit touch to hand holding and good-night kisses.

6. After the reasonable period of time, with wise counsel, if God's leading is not clear, go back to being friends. This may be extremely difficult, but remember: God is in control of your emotions, if you will submit to Him.

I've worked with enough singles to know that some of you reading this will be saying by now, "This guy is crazy if he thinks this is possible in our culture." It's not—without Christ. God has called us as His people to be radically different, in every aspect of our personal relationships. We are not part of the culture. We are not accountable to "society." We belong to Jesus Christ, and we obey Him in *His* culture, His church. As a counselor, I deal with real lives and real struggles. I know God wants godliness in both single people and married people.

Only a framework like this places relationships under His control.

Handling your dating commitments in this way is not only God's will. The process is also best from a human point of view. This perspective will save you from the terrible emotional traumas that devastate or destroy lives.

Every single person must decide, "Am I going to trust God with my dating life?" Where I see singles *wisely* take these principles into dating, tremendous blessings result.

How can a single stay out of trouble in dating? By staying out of the gray zone and by letting God's will be manifest.

Moving On Toward Marriage

Sid had come through ten years of confusion concerning marriage. Four different times he had become infatuated, only to see his feelings dissipate into frustration and uncertainty. All of the young women he dated were exceptional in almost all respects. Still, Sid could never seem to find the confidence to follow through and get married. At age thirty-three, Sid began seriously wondering if something was wrong with him.

Larry and Phyllis, on the other hand, after just five dates, were so emotionally attached that they were embarrassing to be around. After the second date, there had been no question: This was it. The wedding was set for two months away.

Most single people have experienced at least one relationship that caused them to wonder if they should get married. These two cases illustrate the wide range of approaches and experiences. This is why I am calling you to godly sanity and balance. Apart from God, the decision to get married is a hit or miss proposition. For the spiritually committed there are definite roadsigns to a mature decision.

Since we have primarily discussed singleness in this book, let me devote a few pages at the close of this chapter to some insights on moving toward marriage, should God say "yes."

Making Decisions

Making decisions is not easy, and marriage is an extremely difficult, significant decision. The following are some reasons why people struggle in making a decision to marry a certain someone.

1. The timing isn't "right."
2. A partner truly is called to be single.
3. A subconscious fear of marriage.
4. A general problem making decisions.
5. A lack of proper love modeling in the past.
6. A strong independent personality.
7. An overly perfectionistic personality.
8. Too much momentary outside pressure.

Some of these reasons indicate a problem that can be overcome. God is bigger than any of our hang-ups, and spiritual counsel is often helpful.

The important truth to remember in the midst of dating decisions is that God is the one who brings people together, and He will give you peace to marry as well as to stay single.

Maturity

Singles ask me all the time if I can ever be *sure* a given marriage will work. The closest I can come to saying that it can is related to the past history of both partners in the relationship. If both partners have demonstrated maturity in most areas of adult life, then one can more reasonably deduce that they will do well in new responsibilities. Conversely, the less evidence of maturity there is in their track record, the greater the risk.

Let me illustrate. Barbara, who is twenty years old, is trying to make a decision whether or not to marry Bill. Elizabeth, who is twenty-five, is trying to make a decision about marrying Barry. Consider each man's experience in life.

Bill is a twenty-year-old college student with one year left before graduation. Both parents are willing to continue educational support after marriage for the last year of school. Bill became a Christian at eighteen and has been faithful in his pursuit of maturity. He has worked for his Dad's business during the summers since high school and is hoping to get a job with the government after graduation.

Barry, twenty-nine, has been working in commercial real estate for seven years. His business success has just allowed him to buy his first home. He has been a Christian for eight years. Barry leads a men's Bible study and is a board member of a local Christian organization.

Barry certainly offers a better track record in the area of responsibility, and he has logged more time as a Christian. Neither man is necessarily ready for marriage. Yet, the *risk* with Barry appears to be markedly less. Maturity is a highly important factor in a successful marriage. This is not to say, however, that a younger couple sure of God's calling cannot build a godly relationship. God has His own unique plan for each couple headed for marriage. But maturity is an important issue to think about, talk about, and pray about together.

Younger couples struggle more because neither mate has faced life's inevitable problems—work, financial debt, time pressures, and the adult crisis of self-worth. As these and other realities of life hit, each mate will suffer. Often partners blame their individual frustrations and growing pains on the marriage. Many young couples never recover from this period.

The more life issues that have been dealt with over the longest possible time, the lower the risk.

Chronological age is not necessarily the pivotal factor. An older person who is a new Christian tends to be further along in working through life issues but may still be immature in spiritual matters. A younger person may be short on life issues but have a solid, experienced relationship with God. In this case the younger person may be better prepared for marriage.

Faith Perspectives

The second important guideline in determining God's will for marriage is honestly seeking God's will. I realize that many singles "forget" to look at this point. But doing this is the only hope of rising above natural human instinct to a secure relationship that can stand the test of time.

Dating did not exist in biblical times (it's *horribly* modern), so children didn't struggle with the system. Children trusted their parents and God and married without high feeling. Instead of feelings, the young singles had a high consciousness of being in God's will. Therefore, while their proverbial "emotional pot" might have been cold at the point of marriage, the young couple knew the pot would gain warmth from that point forward. Today, couples marry with their pot too hot to handle. With no lasting sense of commitment to God's will, they spend the rest of their married lives letting the pot cool off.

Obviously, most singles use the current dating system, and most would never submit to the old system. Additionally, there are some parents who would choke on the idea of being instruments to help determine God's will. Therefore, let me propose a plan of determining God's will by faith. The plan requires three vital ingredients.

First, the couple must be *accountable* to a mature person in their church or a wise counselor whose perspective on marriage comes from God's Word. Second, both individuals must have established their *maturity* in being faithful to God's will. Third, the couple should be studying God's plan for marriage so that they can evaluate their commitment in light of God's Word.

After truly seeking God's will through these channels, the final confirming factor of God's will for marriage will be the presence of *peace* about the marriage. That deep peace within will be evidence of each individual truly understanding their personal responsibility and the cost factor of godly marriage. The wise counselor's verification of that peace helps seal God's will. I am convinced that when two mature people still have peace to marry after fully understanding the biblical issues in the midst of wise counsel, then God's will can be clearly known.*

For your encouragement, remember that God is a God of "yes's" and "no's." He says in His Word we can *know* His will. The Spirit of God speaks through His Word and

---

*For an excellent description of faith read *Faith Is Not a Feeling* by Ney Bailey (San Bernadino, Calif.: Here's Life Publishers, 1978).

uses wise counsel to verify Himself. A firm confidence in knowing God's will is the radical distinction between "faith" marriage and the "feelings" marriage of our modern day culture.*

---

*After seeking out a wise counselor, may I suggest you read my book *Becoming One*. There I deal specifically with the cost factors and our biblical responsibilities in marriage.

11

Reality in Relationships

Lasting, truly satisfying relationships are miracles! Miracles that result from faith and hard work. There are no shortcuts. Tragically, while most people desire the miracle of experiencing a faith relationship, few are willing to pay the price.

While I have experienced great joy in my relationships, God has continued to test and teach me. Relationships involve unbelievable blessing and pain. Blessing encourages faith, but through pain there can be a deeper blessing. When the concepts of a faith relationship are introduced to two people whose relationship is explosive, the faith concepts are in for a severe testing, believe me.

I have learned that it is not enough for us simply to say, "I believe the faith perspective." We must sit down, look at our lives, and decide specifically how to enact faith relationships in every aspect of our day-to-day living. We need goals. Without those specifics, human instinct will win every time.

With this in mind, let me offer some practical thoughts on the subject. No faith relationship will be perfect, and these reminders I hope will lessen the possibility of your being shocked out of your faith perspective.

Disappointment in Relationships

Personal pain, no matter the cause, affects our close relationships. When an unpleasant or distressing incident occurs between our friend and us, our relationship is tested. Will we forget the perspective God has given us on the relationship and walk out? Or will we respond with faith and work through the problem? A mature single will expect to experience some pain in every important relationship. There are particular realities of our sinful nature that will cause misunderstandings, disappointment, and hurt in our relationships. But don't lose heart! Prepare for these. Remember that at any particular point, no relationship is completely equitable. It takes a solid faith perspective to allow God the freedom to work in your and your friend's lives as He did in David's and Jonathan's. Remember, your struggle is not against that person—don't be deceived about that.

Expect Rejection
Inevitably, all of us will encounter a number of relationships in which we give and give and never see lasting results. Our giving spirit may even be misused by the other person. He or she may take advantage of our friendship and love. When this happens we must realize that God is deepening our faith in Him and sharpening our relational skills. The stronger our persistence in faith, the bigger the blessing yet to come. Thank God for these refining experiences. See what He has in store for you.

Expect to Give More
"I heard you say I might end up giving more than I received, but I guess it didn't really sink in." More than one single has made this comment to me. I can't count

the relationships in which I have given ninety percent while receiving only ten percent back. Yet, had I given up at any one point, I never would have discovered the few relationships that have really blessed me —relationships in which I probably receive more than I give.

Remember Jonathan and David when you feel used. People will take advantage of you, but in the long run you will not lose. God will work it out for good (see Rom. 8:28). There are a few long-term relationships in which I continue to make the major sacrifice. So don't be shocked if suddenly it seems like your friend is getting the better end of the deal. In the long run, God will meet your needs according to His will.

Expect Change

"I finally established an important relationship and then he got a new job and moved to Atlanta," a single guy told me recently. Because singles are more mobile in general than married people, they must be prepared for the reality of change when they establish relationships. As single people begin to see the value of relationships, they must consider them a top priority in decisions to move. Realize the rareness and importance of a solid faith relationship.

The one kind of relationship that can survive a move is the covenant relationship. To maintain a relationship at a distance requires a mature faith commitment. Yet I know people who draw great support and strength from such relationships, even at a great distance.

Covenant Relationships Suffer Too

Much like marriage, covenant relationships between single people will experience severe periods of testing. After being hurt or disappointed because of an unusual or unexpected problem, reestablishing nurture and encouragement is always difficult. Reestablishing feelings of closeness is especially hard if you and your friend are geographically separated.

"Making up" is often easy, but rebuilding emotional bridges is a challenge. During these times, remembering that God has given you this relationship is crucial. From a practical standpoint, make an extra effort to spend time alone with that friend to talk, pray, and reestablish communication. Expect the best to be tested, knowing that the struggle involved in working through the problem will prove worth it.

Be Honest With Yourself Concerning Relationships

Another reality of our sinful nature that threatens faith relationships is failure to understand our own motivations. Our culture teaches us to hide our true feelings, and we do. Many times we have tremendous anxieties and honestly do not know why. Seeing a relationship destroyed because one or both parties were not honest is not unusual.

Not long ago a young lady came to see me because of the terrific problem she was having controlling her emotions. Perpetually, outbursts of anger and criticism gave way to depression and tears. Her roommates were about to pull their hair out. In desperation they had told her to get herself under control or she would have to move out.

In probing for the answer, I kept looking for some subconscious need or threat that could possibly be causing such actions. In this young woman's conscious mind, there was no awareness of jealousy or fear of the other roommates. Finally we discovered that subconsciously she really desired the special friendship of one of the girls in the apartment. She was fearful that she would not be liked. Therefore, she felt threatened by the others. This subconscious fear caused her to become critical, and she felt threatened by the least little problem.

After discovering her real motivations and fears, we brought the rest of the roommates in for some warm communication. Overnight, the problem was solved.

Many times we are driven by desires or fears we have never really understood or faced. Let's look at a few of them.

Dependence vs. Control

The beginning of honesty in any relationship is to realize that, humanly speaking, people move in relationships toward one of two directions: dependence or control. Dependence, taken to the extreme, results in people-worship instead of God-dependence. Control taken to the extreme results in manipulating or using the other person.

Evidence arises soon if a relationship is drifting toward overdependence: a deep emotional fear of losing a person's friendship, a tendency to plan life around another person's schedule, an inability to seek a life of dependence on God apart from the other's approval, and an inability to pursue other relationships. Control or dominance is evidenced by using people for personal benefit, being able to hurt or condemn another person without qualms, or using emotional manipulation on a person to get one's way. All of these symptoms are destructive and impede spiritual growth.

The first step to correct these patterns of relating is to recognize and admit the problem. These struggles can be dealt with if they are identified properly. If left uncon-

fronted, they can destroy more than one life. Make
yourself accountable to a wise counselor if either tendency is evident in your life.

Know Yourself

There are numerous reasons a single person might
pursue a relationship with another single: material benefits, social benefits, political benefits, sexual benefits,
emotional benefits, spiritual benefits, physical safety,
and a calling by God. This list seems simple enough, but
some singles have a very hard time being honest with
themselves concerning their motives for seeking relationships. Being successful in relationships is impossible
if one is not willing to be honest concerning his or her
needs or motives. The following incident illustrates this.

An attractive single man had become very unpopular
with a particular group of women. He was being accused
of being two-faced and overly aggressive sexually. Yet
he was most likeable and had a winning personality.

Several of the young women had mentioned this
man's history to me, so I was not surprised when he
came to see me. As we talked about his track record in
dating, I saw clearly that he was not only fickle but dated
exclusively what he referred to as the "lovely" women.
At first he adamantly denied any possibility that sexual
interest was important to him. It was not until he finally
admitted his sexual needs and motivations that we
began to make progress.

Only as singles admit their true needs and motives in
entering relationships can God fulfill those needs and
motives His way. Singles who have not uncovered and
dealt with their underlying needs and motives honestly,
no matter how proper or improper, are going to continu-

·ally make social blunders, hurt people, and isolate themselves. Once a person is honest with himself about why he is initiating a relationship, he can begin to approach the relationship carefully, knowing his own strengths and weaknesses.

Let's say the purpose for initiating a relationship is the desire for social contact. Obviously this desire could be distorted into a sinful attitude—the desire to be seen in the right places or with a handsome partner. That would need to be dealt with, but there are also healthy, godly reasons for desiring social contact. By admitting that their dating is for the purpose of getting out and having fun both people should be protected from painful misunderstandings. However, refusing to admit and communicate true motives usually means one person will be used and the other will become deceitful and feel cornered or guilty.

Developing Creativity in Relationships

Most singles would say that they desire in-depth relationships. Yet if you look closely at their lives and schedules, they do very little to encourage consistent, time-consuming commitments. In fact, many people actually work against deep relationships by their lifestyles. Every single who understands the value of friendships must develop a creative strategy to develop relationships.

The popularity of soap operas and paperback romances has exploded in the last ten years. Counselors all over America know why. People live out their fantasies and emotions through these fictional stories. A hard run at life itself is too painful, so they live life through fantasies. In so doing, they can have the person they want, do the things they want, and never fail or experience rejection.

Unbelievable, you say? Well, just try to take the soaps off TV! That is not to say that every person who watches soap operas is trying to escape reality. The point is that, generally speaking, people tend to withdraw from relational activities when they encounter pain and rejection. Only God can provide the insight necessary to overcome this withdrawal. The following points of wisdom are vital, practical steps in the process.

Emphasize Your Strengths

"Nobody really likes me. I don't belong. I am too quiet and I feel so uncomfortable in groups," Pat shared in counseling. Her tone indicated she was trying to convince herself as much as me. Many singles I meet are convinced of their weaknesses but very uncertain about their strengths. They believe they are second-class citizens because they are not married, and without realizing it, they communicate the same inferiority feelings to others.

I spend over half my counseling undoing false beliefs, before I can help create a true, biblical belief in one's self. Pat is a good example. She was very talented musically and had a fine singing voice. In addition, she had taken over five years of lessons in gymnastics, and she enjoyed snow skiing and ice skating. She possessed excellent writing talents and could type over eighty words a minute. She loved doing things for close friends and was known as an encourager.

In one hour we came up with twenty-five different possibilities for involvement with people that would emphasize her strengths. We isolated five of the most attractive possibilities, and within two weeks, three of these five became realities.

In most cases, social defeat is ninety percent in one's mind. The first step in winning the battle of self-image is to seek a wise friend to help index and categorize your interests and strengths. Then, as the Lord places you with other people, be sensitive, where possible, to match your personality and strengths with the personality and strengths that blend and support yours. I have noticed that God consistently provides me with people whom I can strengthen and who also make me stronger.

If I am placed with several people, I am automatically attracted to those with strengths unlike mine—strengths I need to complete me. The thought is not to exclude others but, where spiritually legitimate, to emphasize those relationships that encourage you.

As you come to see your strengths, develop relational habits. If you're a reader, don't always sit in the bedroom alone; occasionally go to the library with people. Develop the hobbies *you're* interested in—skiing, bridge, scuba diving, jogging, painting—but do them with people.

Bible studies, retreats, church groups, and community service projects are also good examples of activities that create relational experiences. Many singles retreat into isolation because of a lack of self-confidence. Then they become bored and uninteresting, which isolates them further. (No one likes to get to know a dull person!) This is a vicious cycle—so don't let this happen to you. Organize relational experiences. If such an aggressive step is not your style, invite someone who likes to organize over for dinner and encourage him to organize for you. It *is* amazing what a little strategy will do in establishing strong relationships.

Know Your Liabilities

A single man I counseled with named Lewis asked me to help him improve his ability to relate to others. After a few meetings I asked him what he considered to be his liabilities—personality traits that might make relating difficult. He really had no solid grasp of what they were, so we set about to discover them.

I asked him to observe closely others' responses to him for several weeks. Then I asked him to select the people who knew him best, one from each of five areas of life: work, living environment, spiritual life, dating life, and his best friend (of the same sex). We made up a brief, simple questionnaire for each of the five to fill out, rating Lewis on a scale of 1–10 (see chart on following page).

After identifying his liabilities, we were able to begin offsetting them more easily.

Recognize the Value of Others

Many times singles are so self-centered and determined to express themselves that they lose sight of their friends' needs for self-worth. A lasting relationship requires that *both* parties experience freedom of expression and a sense of value. Without mutual value, the relationship will eventually self-destruct. Blessed is the single who discovers the joy of building a friend's self-image; that single is very important to others.

The first step in recognizing another person's value is unconditional acceptance of that person. The faith principles covered earlier are the biblical requisites for accepting people as they are. Realize that, as you apply these faith principles, God can match your strengths with the other person's weaknesses. Don't let a person's weaknesses shock you. Anticipate them and creatively offset them.

Negative outlook on life	1 2 3 4 5 6 7 8 9 10	Positive outlook on life
Self-conscious personality	1 2 3 4 5 6 7 8 9 10	People-oriented personality
Critical of others	1 2 3 4 5 6 7 8 9 10	Encouraging to others
Loner	1 2 3 4 5 6 7 8 9 10	Very relational
Narrow interests	1 2 3 4 5 6 7 8 9 10	Varied interests
High self-worth	1 2 3 4 5 6 7 8 9 10	Low self-worth
Interest in short-term relationships	1 2 3 4 5 6 7 8 9 10	Interest in long-term relationships
Low spiritual interests	1 2 3 4 5 6 7 8 9 10	High spiritual interests
Tendency toward anger & resentment	1 2 3 4 5 6 7 8 9 10	Tendency toward forgiveness & support
Not trustworthy	1 2 3 4 5 6 7 8 9 10	Highly trustworthy

List one positive concerning Lewis' ability to establish meaningful relationships.

List one negative concerning Lewis' ability to establish meaningful relationships.

As an example, I have a good friend who is an excellent Bible teacher. However, this friend has an abrasive personality that occasionally offends people. Since the Lord has given me a gift of dealing skillfully with people, I decided to ask the man if he wanted to team-teach a series with me. The results were exciting. Our strengths and weaknesses complemented each other's, resulting in a more effective teaching experience.

Over the years I have become convinced that the greatest talent a person can have is the ability to observe value in others. Charting a friend on the preceding questionnaire might give you a hint about how to discern his or her strengths.

If you care enough to take the time to discover every hidden talent and strength of a friend, you will both be blessed. I am persuaded that I should be just as purposeful with my friend's gifts and talents as I am with my own. If you set the same goal, you will find that you are a good friend for someone else to have.

Monitor Painful Relationships

God expects all people, singles included, to look at Him as the Source and Provider of their relationships. He expects us to "faint not," but to persevere in our responsibility to love others, imperfect as we are. Yet He also wants us to be careful of relationships that bring prolonged pain to the participants.

Some painful relationships we know are ultimately good for us, in spite of the pain. We know we are learning valuable lessons. On the other hand, there are painful relationships that clearly are not from God. When consistently sinful actions and thoughts are the fruit and you know you are being torn spiritually, God wants you out of that relationship.

Such involvements are extremely difficult—and dangerous. Seek wise counsel from others regularly concerning these relationships. God may be teaching you something by leaving you in a burdensome relationship. But it may also be God's will to terminate the friendship.

Summary

Singles need family too! Relationships are God's way of putting physical arms around you and me.

My desire? To motivate you to discover the family God has placed you in, in order that He might meet the "aloneness" need He created in you. Vital relationships are necessities, not options, for singles. Commit today to begin finding God's provision for you.

PART III

THE PURPOSEFUL
SINGLE LIFE

12

Free to Be Purposeful

As Ed pulled his arm back from turning off the lamp, he could feel his body relax for the first time since 6:00 that morning. The bed felt great tonight, but as good as it felt, it didn't compare with the excitement and satisfaction Ed felt about life in general—and particularly about the day just ending.

A mile jog was all he had had time for that morning because of a breakfast appointment at 7:00 with a good friend. Ed wanted to have plenty of time in prayer before meeting with Dave, who was having some personal problems. They had been meeting for several weeks to talk about possible solutions to Dave's difficulties.

After breakfast, on the way to work, Ed stopped off at a printer to pick up copies of a presentation he was to make at the office that day. The presentation would explain an exciting new business concept he had been working on for several months. If the company leadership responded positively, he would be the one to put the plan into action. What a challenge!

At noon he took a new friend to a men's luncheon to hear another businessman share about his relationship with Jesus Christ. Back at the office, Ed made his presentation. His colleagues were intrigued, but they needed time to consider the plan.

Later that afternoon Ed joined three men from his church to discuss plans to work with inner-city youth. They hoped to involve people from several churches on Saturday mornings starting in September.

At 7:30 that evening, Ed picked up Margie and went to a discussion group he was leading. Afterwards several friends stopped by his house, which they had not seen since Ed had finished his restoration project. His dream of renovating an older home had finally been realized.

The room was dark now, and Ed was fading fast. His last fleeting thoughts were, *Lord, I've got a lot to do tomorrow. Thank You for today.*

The last major section of this book is designed to persuade you that singles must be purposeful with their lives. Whether male or female, young or old, outgoing or reserved, educated or not, God does not intend for any life to be wasted. Single people should prepare themselves for responsibilities in the church, in business, in government, and in virtually every activity of life.

If you think about it, Ed's life encompassed being a counselor, a businessman, a teacher, a leader, a friend, a homeowner, as well as a minister. No wonder Ed was excited. His life was full! Even though individual strengths and gifts vary greatly, everyone needs to experience life as fully as one's abilities allow.

Every single person needs to exercise authority and experience ownership. He or she should learn how to counsel and teach as well as how to protect and provide in any given relationship. The single person also must learn to submit to authority and to cultivate generosity. He or she should be able to demonstrate and receive affection, compassion, and vulnerability in relationships. When? Not next year, not after marriage, not after financial security, not even after becoming "mature." *Now is the time to get on with living.*

Purposeful, meaningful lives, like successful relationships, don't just happen. They are made. They are formed. They are developed.

When I look for help in the successful planning of my life, I look to older men and women who have demonstrated what I am after. I need *models*. What do these Christians have to say? One such person is the apostle Paul. Consider his words to the young man, Timothy, written toward the end of Paul's life.

> No soldier in active service entangles himself in the affairs of everyday life, so that he may please the one who enlisted him as a soldier. And also if anyone competes as an athlete, he does not win the prize unless he competes according to the rules. The hard-working farmer ought to be the first to receive his share of the crops (2 Tim. 2:4–6).

Paul challenged Timothy to approach his life as a soldier, as an athlete, and as a farmer. What qualities are associated with these vocations? Courage, faithfulness, single-mindedness, and discipline—these were the qualities Paul wanted to see in Timothy. Each one is necessary to your life, too, if you want to experience abundant living.

Paul warned Timothy that he would be confronted with two life-styles to choose from. The same is true for us. The first is one of human self-centeredness, which leads to arrogance, disobedience, gossip, conceit, and love of worldly pleasures (see 2 Tim. 3:1–5). The second life-style is one of wisdom, based on the Word of God. Wisdom is defined as "applied knowledge and skill in living."

Paul's strongest statement comes at the end of the

letter where he solemnly charged Timothy to be prepared at all times to teach Scripture (see 2 Tim. 4:1ff). The Bible is basic to training in godliness and protects us from self-centered life-styles.

Paul told Timothy to endure hardship. Many people allow trials and pain to destroy their lives and their relationships.

Paul exhorted Timothy to fulfill his ministry. The implication is that every person has a ministry responsibility from God's perspective. Do you know what your gifts and talents are and how God would have you use them?

Paul gave three illustrations of success from his own life. First, he said, "I have fought *the good fight*" (2 Tim. 4:7, italics mine). The good fight is the process of living by faith. Paul based his actions and decisions not on human instinct but on God's Word and His promises. Second, he said, "I have *finished the course*" (v.7). Paul believed that there had been a specific plan for his life and that he had completed the course God had opened up to him. Third, he wrote, "I have *kept the faith*" (v.7). You see, Paul had not just learned and taught Christian doctrine, but he had lived and preserved what Scripture taught. He had been faithful to pass on the true faith of Jesus Christ.

Paul concluded by stating his ultimate goal in life. He said, "In the future there is laid up for me the crown of righteousness . . . " (2 Tim. 4:8). Paul's primary motivation was his desire to be with Christ for all eternity. He *knew* a great future inheritance was his! That fact gave Paul the daily strength to finish his task in life. In the end, Paul's life proved that everything pertaining to *life and godliness* is, in fact, in an intimate knowledge of God and His promises.

Paul's exhortations to Timothy are just as relevant in the twentieth century as they were two thousand years ago. You and I must develop a disciplined life-style, seek a life of wisdom by adhering to Scripture, be strong in life's trials, complete our ministries, live by faith rather than feelings, seek God's plan for our lives, live out the biblical faith, and eagerly look forward to heaven and the eternal kingdom.

If we are committed to living a purposeful life, we must, then, determine to develop our character along these scriptural injunctions. How does one begin this task?

The Search for Wholeness

Timothy was not able to develop the qualities necessary for purposeful living all by himself. He needed the church of Jesus Christ. I keep coming back to the church because the church is central to all of Scripture.

In Ephesians 4:4 Paul wrote, "There is one body and one Spirit, just as also you were called in one hope of your calling." From God's perspective you and I are one in the Holy Spirit. The same is true of all believers. Our relationship with God and with His family is where completion ultimately is found. We were called for this purpose: to be built up together in Christ.

Do most singles feel whole and complete? I fear not. The problem, though, is not with God and His provision. What we need, what we are called to is right under our noses! The church has been there for two thousand years, ready to be our home, our family, our foundation —the resource we need to meet our deepest needs. Our problem is, we have not been looking in the right place. For thirty-two years of my life I walked right past the church. It was essentially me and Jesus. And then I discovered the richness that lay in the Body of Christ to meet my needs.

Only as single Christians join with other believers, in mutual submission, will they begin to experience the kind of fulfillment that Paul and Timothy knew. When singles begin to experience relationships that they view as being clearly from the Lord, then they can support each other in the deepest sense. Satan has blinded us to our need for God's church.

For those of you who are in a church but are not being blessed as you had hoped to be, remember that the church is composed of sinners. Even mature Christians err. Don't set yourself up for disillusionment by cultivating the illusion that the church, here and now, is already in its perfected state. New Christians often become cynical and critical of the church when this illusion of theirs is shattered, never realizing that they are being unrealistic, judgmental, and unloving.

No local body of Christians will be perfect or live up to your ideals. But God calls you to take your place in the Body of Christ; He tells you not to forsake assembling together with other believers; and so to be obedient to Him you really have no choice but to seek out that group of believers with whom God would have you serve and worship Him. By doing this, you may not necessarily *feel* completed right away, nor will you automatically lose your desire for a mate, or find one. But as you give yourself to God and His people, *in commitment, in love, and in submission*, the practical outworking of your completion in Christ will be set in action.

If you have not yet done so, make a commitment today to seek out a vital Christ-centered church experience. Seek a group of believers who demonstrate the kind of oneness in Christ that encourages and blesses you. *Choose to believe* that God's church is vital to your faith and life.

Accountability

Most growing Christians recognize their spiritual need to be held accountable for their actions and to be encouraged to do good works. Single people need the church for these very reasons. The church serves, in part, as an anchor in this world to protect spiritual life and vision from going adrift.

The word *single* implies isolation, and isolation proves problematic. It is not part of God's plan. From Genesis to Revelation, we see God developing relationships between individuals. From God's perspective, every Christian—married or single—is accountable to God and to those people whom God places around him. Singles especially experience severe problems when isolated from the protection of Christian relationships.

Remember: "Without consultation, plans are frustrated, /But with many counselors, they succeed" (Prov. 15:22), and "Be subject to one another in the fear of Christ" (Eph. 5:21). I repeat: *Isolation from others is dangerous and is not a part of God's plan.*

Timothy and Paul's relationship is a model of how a younger Christian can submit to and learn from an older and more mature believer. Paul was able to exhort, instruct, protect, and love his younger friend. Paul also mentioned Timothy's relationships with his Christian mother and grandmother as being extremely important in Timothy's spiritual development.

Every single Christian should commit himself or herself to several individuals in the church whom God can use to protect the believer against wrong decisions and unwise involvement. The church is the best place to look for spiritually mature men and women. You may first evaluate these individuals by the measure established in Scripture for spiritual leadership (see Tit. 1 and 1 Tim. 3).

Sometimes godly men and women who have known and loved you over a number of years and who fit these qualifications might be better suited than your own church leaders. However, in the right church, your responsibility is first to your elders. Long-term, consistent evaluation of and submission to such counsel will prove invaluable over a lifetime. The following story illustrates what can happen when such counsel is not sought.

A frustrated and confused single man sat waiting for my response to his story. A thousand questions filled my mind. How had he decided to change jobs three times in five years, attend four different churches, and live in six apartments with eight different roommates? How could an intelligent human being put himself through that struggle? Just the thought made me tired!

At twenty-eight years old, with two years in the army and five years in business behind him, this man had no idea where he was headed or what to do next. Few definite signs of life goals or strengths were surfacing. To a great extent, his life was an accumulation of decisions based on momentary instincts and fantasies. Wise counsel from a mature believer over the years could have shown the way of truth to this young man and made the difference between his confusing plight and a fulfilled and Spirit-directed life.

Job changes, moves, major business decisions, and marriage are primary examples of those decisions that should be prayed through with a godly counselor in the local church where Christ has placed you. The value of God's system of accountability is immeasurable when singles allow it to work.

When change for the sake of change tempts us to live and make decisions independent of counsel, we leave ourselves open to confusion, loneliness, instability, and a host of other problems. Some single people will eventually seek professional counseling, but such attempts often are useless, because the counselor doesn't know the person well enough. I say that as a counselor! God's plan for counsel within the church is best in these cases.

A word of caution proves wise at this point. There is a difference between spiritual counsel and "control." I am not talking about becoming robots here. Control oppresses, discourages, and becomes legalistic. Spiritual direction, on the other hand, encourages, supports and frees the person involved. An individual never loses his or her direct accountability to God and His Word (whereas control tries to take over that relationship). Counsel should support God's will and purpose for His people and *never* contradict God's written Word.

For an excellent description of how the church can function, I recommend the book *Sharpening the Focus of the Church* by Gene Getz and *Body Life* by Ray Stedman. Being held accountable, nurture from God's Word, relationships, vision, and opportunities to serve are just a few of the vital life resources the true church offers. Being truly purposeful in life begins with establishing your place in Christ's Body.

Honoring Our Parents

So far I have not addressed the relationship of the single person to his or her parents. However, I believe that for a single to be *free* to be purposeful, he or she needs to face this issue squarely and biblically.

Often single people find themselves either too dependent upon or too independent from their parents. Of course, parents may be responsible in part for creating these conditions by either exercising too much control over their adult children's lives or by refusing even to lend a hand because of the mistaken idea that self-sufficiency is a virtue. (No one is totally self-sufficient, nor should we be.)

The Bible tells us to honor our parents, and the promise of long life is attached to that command (see Ex. 20:12). In Proverbs 15:20, we read, "A wise son makes a father glad,/But a foolish man despises his mother." Even as adults we are to honor our parents by listening respectfully to their advice and seeking their counsel. We are to demonstrate love for them by keeping in touch regularly, being interested in their lives, preparing ourselves to care for them if that becomes necessary, and *allowing* them to love us in the only way they can—as parents.

If your relationship with your parents has not been a good one, you need to examine your own heart and determine what you have done to contribute to the conflicts. Ask the Lord for true repentance and then seek His forgiveness. You may need to approach your parents and ask them for forgiveness. This will be extremely difficult, especially if they have hurt you. But as Christians we are to "pursue peace with all men" (Heb. 12:14), and that includes parents.

An important point: *We are to honor and respect our parents even if we think they don't deserve it.* This is a matter of obedience to the Lord, lived out by faith.

Another thing to remember is that honoring our parents is not always the same as obeying them. Children (those who are dependent) are to obey their parents. This is God's command. So long as you are being supported largely by your parents, I believe you are obligated under God to be subject to them. But if you are financially independent and living away from your parents' home (or helping with living expenses and responsibilities in the home), I believe you should make a conscious decision to leave parental authority and "cleave" to Christ in His Body, the church. Even then, though, your obedience to your parents should be replaced by deep honor and respect.

Let me be very practical here. A good friend has a father who has a "sixth sense" when it comes to purchasing a home or a car. My friend is committed to following his father's counsel in these areas. The older man simply knows more and has protected his son from more than one raw deal. And what honor and respect there is between them! Learn to lean on the wisdom of those who brought you life.

Begin to Live—Now

Freedom to live a full and contented life *now* cannot be realized until you determine not to live in the future. As you learn to function in Christ's Body, as you test your thoughts and plans with godly counselors, I believe you will begin to find out that life *right now* can be pretty rewarding. Many forces—the world, our own sinfulness, and the Devil—will try to keep you in bondage. Being aware of these forces and the manifestations of their influence is the subject of the next chapter.

13

Freedom Robbers

As David left my office, my frustration at not being able to help him was almost unbearable. I wanted to relieve his depression, but every suggestion I offered was met with unwillingness.

David had allowed himself to be entrapped by a worldly mess. He was in debt, resulting in a terrible credit rating. Between working two jobs, helping with a political campaign, and playing on two softball teams, David had only two or three nights a month free. He couldn't afford anything, people constantly were reflecting disappointment in him, and he had no time to develop relationships.

Single people who live solely to fulfill their ever-changing natural desires and appetites will inevitably lead chaotic, frustrated, and lonely lives. Christian singles, however, who determine to live by faith in God often will be frustrated also, because of the powerful influence of sin in and around them. This influence is often subtle, and therein lies its danger. The freedom to live a purposeful life can be severely, even totally, limited by sin and its effects.

In this chapter, I want to address certain sinful tendencies common to all people, and how single people in particular can be affected if they do not hold these tendencies in check. Balance and moderation are the keys in most cases.

The Time War

Perhaps the best way to determine whether you are in trouble spiritually (which colors every other area of life) is to evaluate how you spend your time. We all fight a continual battle to protect ourselves from habits and tendencies that in the long run become destructive. Even good activities can be overdone and lead to an imbalanced life.

Scripture warns us to be sensitive to our use of time.

> Therefore be careful how you walk, not as unwise men, but as wise, making the most of your time, for the days are evil (Eph. 5:15,16).

Paul knew that Christians are in a battle for their spiritual lives. Getting involved in a life-style that does not allow for personal contact with God and His people is spiritual suicide, cut short only by God's mercy and faithfulness.

David, the single man mentioned earlier, had become too busy to spend time with God. No wonder he was depressed! He seemed not to realize he was wide open for Satan's attacks as a result of his negligence.

Another crucial need David was not facing up to was his need for good friends. He knew lots of people, but he was not willing, or able perhaps, to get to know any of them beyond the superficial level. The main reason for this, though, was his hectic schedule. *Building relationships takes time*.

Single people who are not consciously trying to live

balanced lives have a tendency to move in one of two directions when it comes to use of time. Some, like David, fill up all their free time with various activities, which by themselves are not necessarily bad. Taken together, though, they begin to take priority over everything else, leaving the person at the mercy of his or her own poorly planned schedule. As usual, it's easier to get involved in these activities and commitments than it is to get out of them. But if freedom to live purposefully is to be regained, the person in this situation *must* determine to seek God's leading and reorder priorities accordingly.

The other extreme is the single person who becomes a virtual recluse. He or she has no social or community involvements, few friends, rarely travels except to and from work, and is selfish with time. This person has become accustomed to doing things alone and usually prefers it that way. People like this eat when and what they like, read or watch TV as they please, live as neatly or as sloppily as they prefer, and use other people only to alleviate occasional loneliness. Self-indulgence and laziness often become a way of life. They really believe they need only live to please themselves. Actually, though, such people are often bored with life, depressed, and introspective. Change can come only when a person recognizes the rut he or she is in and determines to plan, prayerfully, ways to reach out to other people in service.

Most single people probably are at least aware of these two dangerous extremes and their own tendency to move in the direction of one or the other. Maintaining balance takes conscious, planned effort. Spiritual counsel from more mature believers can certainly help one establish balance in this area of godly time management. Accountability such as this will help to guard against "walking unwisely" in these evil times.

In the World and of the World

The tendency to misuse time is influenced greatly by our attitude toward God's Word. If we habitually neglect what God has revealed of Himself, we will lead disobedient lives. It's as simple as that. But most growing Christians know that and are struggling constantly to give priority to God and His ways.

When explaining the parable of the sower to His disciples, Jesus listed three results of the Fall that cause people to ignore what God has said, leaving their lives barren.

> *The worries of the world*, and *the deceitfulness of riches*, and *the desires for other things* enter in and choke the word, and it becomes unfruitful (Mark 4:19, italics mine).

Under the three categories Christ used, I want to briefly discuss major traps that pull singles away from God's perspective as revealed in His Word. These traps tend to isolate singles from the fellowship of other Christians in the Body of Christ.

Let me warn you before you start that the list you are about to consider is long. Therefore, you may feel that I'm being legalistic at times. Reject such thoughts, because these issues are addressed totally for your protection. Only as you are aware of the dangers can you stay out of traps and maintain a healthy balance in your life. Promoting true freedom, not setting up prohibitions, is the intent of this discussion.

Worries of the World

Have you ever caught yourself feeling nauseous or anxious but you didn't know why? We live in stressful

times. Most people are plagued by fears, either consciously or subconsciously. We fear nuclear holocaust,
political upheavals, the eroding effects of inflation, vio-
lent crimes, catastrophic illnesses, growing old—the list
is endless. These fears and pressures oppress us and
often lead us to over-involvement in causes that, at best,
offer only temporary solutions or momentary post-
ponements.

Because single people often do have more time to
promote various worthwhile causes, they need to guard
against allowing their particular concerns and interests
to replace or take priority over their devotion to Christ.
Even though our faith leads us to be concerned about the
direction of society, we must never forget to maintain a
spiritual perspective, one that views the ultimate solution to sin in this world as the redemption of men and
women—one by one. Let me mention a few examples of
the kind of involvements that can lead us to put faith in
worldly solutions.

Political and Social Causes

Jesus said the poor will always be with us, and He said
this to Judas, His betrayer, who in his supposed concern
for the poor rebuked Mary, the sister of Lazarus, for
anointing Jesus with costly ointment (see John 12:3–8).
Obviously, Jesus was not indifferent to the poor. But the
principle here, I believe, has to do with motives. Mary's
motive was her love and devotion to her Lord. Judas's
motive was one of self-righteous pride and greed.

I have talked to many people who live in Washington,
D.C. Ambitious singles from all over the country come
here with hopes of making a significant contribution to
society. Before they know it, they're caught up in the

thrill and prestige of the political limelight. Initially it begins with just a campaign; then the opportunity comes to "join the staff." The temptation to put aside personal devotion to God and spiritual concerns such as evangelism is great. Many yield to the temptation, only to turn up a few years later spiritually weak, disillusioned by the political process (which they wrongly expected too much of), and less inclined to commit themselves to *any* cause.

Singles who are not directly involved in the party process may become advocates or opponents of certain social reforms. I personally am very interested in causes that affect the family. We can and should effect changes that alleviate human suffering. Corporate sin should be exposed, not winked at. But for all our efforts we need to realize that sin originates in the human heart. We need to give priority to those activities (like prayer) that we know without doubt Jesus has called us to so that our efforts will not be in vain.

Most importantly, Christians ought not to despair. As we see this world passing away, headed for Christ's return, we must remember that our only hope is in Jesus Christ. What a great hope that is! Sharing the gospel of the eternal kingdom must not be neglected.

We may need to examine our motives for wanting to improve society when we don't even show love for our own unbelieving neighbors. For all our religious rhetoric that says we're fighting against this or that to glorify God, are we not sometimes merely trying to protect a comfortable way of life? We must be open to God's leading in the social and political realms, but we ought not to use His name as a means to justify our fears, worries, and temporal solutions.

Health Concerns and Aging

The fear of catastrophic illnesses such as cancer and heart disease has led many to join health spas, to diet, to buy vitamins, to eat so-called "health" foods, and to do anything to eliminate stress, which is being blamed as a significant contributing factor to such illnesses.

I believe we ought to take care of our physical bodies in the best way we know how so that we can better serve the Lord. This will take a certain amount of time and effort. But I don't believe we should live as if lengthening our life span is our primary concern. Avoiding physical pain and the dying process is, of course, impossible.

Single people who become over-concerned with their health or with maintaining a youthful appearance may find themselves thinking of little else. Their activities and social concerns may all tie in with this obsession, which could stem from fear of death or fear of ultimately facing pain and death alone. A related fear could be that age will eliminate the opportunity for marriage. No single woman wants to be labeled a "spinster" or an "old maid."

This particular "worry of the world" can lead to spiritual paralysis. It's an especially self-centered concern that tends to limit time spent in showing concern for others. Rather, time is spent in trying to "save my life" instead of losing it for Jesus' sake. Perhaps the best solution to the dilemma is for the single person to talk about his or her concern with a trained counselor with the purpose of pinpointing the fear behind the concern. A thorough physical examination could also help provide assurance that all is well.

Gossip

This may seem like an odd category under "worries of

the world," but actually it's quite fitting. Gossip usually stems from the desire to appear "in the know" and to feel as if we're better than the person we're criticizing. Of course, Christians often use gossip to make themselves sound truly concerned about someone else's sin or misfortune. The "worry" that gossipers have become obsessed with is other people's business and their own image. Gossip destroys relationships, if it is listened to eagerly. *The one who gossips and the one who listens are equally at fault.*

Singles may resist the notion that they are gossips, but, believe me, anyone can be a gossip. Have you ever heard statements like these: "Did you know Sue is divorced?" "I can't believe Mary is dating him. I thought she had more sense than that." "My boss is incompetent and lazy, and to top it off he's having an affair with my secretary!" "I'd just like for all of you to pray for Jim. He's really struggling with a drinking problem that he doesn't want anyone to know about, but I feel as if you need to know so that you can pray for him more intelligently."

The tendency to gossip is so subtle. If you hold grudges or tend to be critical, you may be involved in gossiping without thinking of it as such. People usually become aware quickly of who thrives on gossip—and they learn to avoid such people. Ultimately, the gossiper's spiritual life is negatively affected.

The Deceitfulness of Riches

The major objective of the advertising industry is to cause you and me to be dissatisfied with what we have. We are enticed to buy every imaginable gadget and philosophy: a new car, a video recorder, a new suit, a trip, a new body, more beautiful hair, and better sex.

When a product is no longer new, it suddenly becomes "improved."

Years ago, the power of this advertising assault was brought home to me when the first word out of my baby daughter's mouth was "Mac's," as she pointed to the yellow arches of a McDonald's restaurant.

We can expect to be vulnerable to imbalance in our lives because of this materialistic programming. Wealth need not be evil, but our attitude toward it may be. The apostle James said this about the love of riches in James 5:1–3:

> Come now, you rich, weep and howl for your miseries which are coming upon you. Your riches have rotted and your garments have become moth-eaten. Your gold and your silver have rusted; and their rust will be a witness against you and will consume your flesh like fire. It is in the last days that you have stored up your treasure!

The amassing of possessions is very destructive to an individual's life. The drain on time and energy, the calloused attitudes toward people who are "in the way," the unfortunate appetites that are bred, and the fear and pain felt when wealth perishes—the acquisition of wealth can leave a track of destruction. Evaluate your own pursuit of riches regularly. Is it controlling you? How is it affecting you and those around you? Seek a plan of restraint and balance.

Workaholics

When there are no limits on personal freedom, it becomes easy for single people to become wrapped up in their job or profession. Many times employers misuse or take advantage of single people for this very reason. A person suffering from a poor self-image feeds on office praise and will do almost anything to continue receiving it. Do not allow your life to be your job. Work can be addictive to the point that nothing else seems to satisfy. Getting raises and bonuses is good for your morale, but what good is extra income if you don't take time to manage it wisely or if accumulating money is your only goal?

Hard work is a real blessing, but even God rested on the seventh day! If you average more than fifty hours a week on the job over a month's time, it may be God's will, but seeking counsel to verify that fact is important. How balanced is your life? How well do you know God? How many lasting relationships are you building? Don't sacrifice eternal rewards for temporal success and financial security.

Ruthlessness

When a person begins to make significant amounts of money, a variety of sensations occur. Power, selfishness, greed—generosity and the desire to help the helpless—all sorts of positive and negative inclinations surface. The love of money is a powerful force. As God blesses you financially, be aware of the spiritual, moral, and relational pitfalls that come with money's charm.

The term that perhaps best describes the evil inherent in lovers of money is *ruthlessness*. Ruthlessness can be spotted first in one's attitude toward making money. Disrespect, manipulation, and dishonesty are rampant in the business and professional arena today.

Christian businessmen often throw their Christian ethics and compassion aside because of greed. Recently I was listening to a "Christian" salesman. He talked about the buying public as if we were gullible fools, about his competitors as if they were vicious dogs, and about his bosses as if they were insensitive thieves. The anger and guile in this person's life was destroying his Christian spirit.

Do not become ruthless in business! As a Christian, you are to work hard and do your best, leaving it to God to advance you and bless you. You are to love and respect others, even those who may be promoted instead of you. Your clients or customers are people whom you are to *serve* with kindness and fairness. Good business ethics are not optional. Obedience to God and His Word is required of you even in the marketplace—even if it costs you your job.

Bad Investments

Nothing entraps quicker or tears at the heart and spirit more than to be cheated or misled financially. All of us are vulnerable to attractive deals.

Who hasn't, at one time or another, gotten involved in a buy-on-time deal? Health club memberships, cars, magazine and tape clubs, furniture, vacuum cleaners, pots and pans, and vacations deals come to mind. How many times have you purchased such an item without really knowing the product, only to be disillusioned later? Only by then, you're stuck with the payments. Never buy something impulsively. Research the product (*Consumer Reports* is available in most libraries), think and pray about making the purchase, compare products, *then* make a decision. Chances are, your desire to buy the product will wane, and you'll discover you don't even need it.

Major purchases, such as insurance, stocks, and real estate, need to be made thoughtfully and cautiously. A mistake in one of these areas can result in financial loss that could encumber you for years, if not for a lifetime.

Again, you need to do your homework. Talk to *veterans* in these fields, (preferably to those who have been in the business for over ten years) both to buyers and sellers. Don't just talk to one or two, but talk to several people. Do some reading. Learn what the risks are. Pray. Making major purchases properly is simply hard work. Don't think God doesn't expect you to use your head. He has called us to be good stewards.

Certainly every business opportunity carries risk, and I hope you will be a little daring occasionally. But I trust you will seriously consider the downside realities and prepare accordingly. The result will be protection from bankruptcy and financial frustrations that inevitably impede life and spiritual development.

The "deceitfulness of riches" robs many people of a potentially meaningful life. The Word of God is unable to bear fruit in these individuals because their pursuits lead them away from God. Paul in 1 Timothy 6:10 said it this way:

> For the love of money is a root of all sorts of evil, and some by longing for it, have wandered away from the faith, and pierced themselves with many a pang.

Every financial dealing must be looked upon as a potential snare of the Evil One.

We must establish a godly balance in our financial lives. The writer of Proverbs 30:8 prayed for this condition:

> . . . Give me neither poverty nor riches;
> Feed me with the food that is my portion,
> Lest I be full and deny Thee and say, "Who is the LORD?"
> Or lest I be in want and steal,
> And profane the name of my God.

Moderation in all things is the key to a proper attitude toward money and possessions. If we do not realize our daily dependence upon and need for the Lord because of false financial security, we are denying the Lord. Likewise, if we allow financial insecurity to keep us from trusting the Lord for His provision, we are profaning His name.

Financial Giving

The last thought on the deceitfulness of riches is a positive one. The best protection anyone can have in financial matters is to become a generous giver. No matter what one makes financially, giving generously —and sacrificially—to people in need and to the cause of Christ, tends to protect against the evils we've discussed. It is hard to be selfish when giving.

Paul actually says the generous giver takes "hold of that which is life indeed."

> Instruct those who are rich in this present world [compared to many in this present world, you *are* rich] not to be conceited or to fix their hope on the uncertainty of riches, but on God, who richly supplies us with all things to enjoy. Instruct them to do good, to be rich in good works, to be generous and ready to share, storing up for themselves the treasure of a good foundation for the future, so that they may take hold of that which is life indeed (1 Tim. 6:17–19).

The Desires for Other Things

What Christ meant by "the desires for other things" (the King James Version says "lusts of other things") could probably be illustrated in many ways. Any inordinate desire or obsession surely would fit in this category, from gluttony to materialism. For our purposes, though, I want to address sexual lust and the quest for pleasure. I believe single people struggle with these temptations perhaps more often than with any others.

Please remember, I am talking about lust—unre-strained, selfish craving—not God-given sexual desires. The desire for sex is not of itself wrong. I am not trying to put anyone under a legalistic pile. Likewise, to experi-ence pleasure is a good thing. But to pursue pleasure at all costs is not good. Again, we're looking for godliness and balance, so that the freedom to live a purposeful life will not be limited.

Sexual Fantasies

Our normal sexual instinct is played upon constantly by the media's sex blitz: books, TV, movies, magazines, and even billboards. Sexual fantasies are no longer a private matter. Now we can live them out vicariously while watching *Days of Our Lives* or *Dallas*. Books, movies, and TV shows create a climate conducive to all kinds of wild fantasies. (Try going a week without TV, and see if your mind trips don't clear up to a degree.) Sexual fantasies can open the door to destruction. If engaged in unchecked, often the opportunity to live out the fantasies is entered into with little resistance. The difference between the fantasy and the reality, though, is stark.

Fantasies lead to false and unrealistic expectations in regard to romance and sex. When the illusions are de-stroyed, introspection and depression result. Still want-ing to experience the fantasy, the person is vulnerable to sinful behavior that blocks spiritual growth, communica-tion with God, and purposeful living.

Recently a very attractive and talented twenty-eight-year-old called me. She was emotionally and physically sick. She cried constantly. *Devastated* is the word that best described her. After just a few minutes, it became apparent that she was fantasizing daily about marriage and romance. Sex was not a big part of her daydreams, but she badly wanted to be loved. The desire was good and normal. The fantasy, however, was destroying her. She was losing perspective, getting mad at God, feeling sorry for herself, and losing her vision in life.

An uncontrolled fantasy life will lead you away from God and His Word. Be honest about your fantasy life. Identify its pattern. Do you fantasize in the morning, during the day, or at night? Determine what usually triggers your fantasies, and avoid the stimulus if you can. Turn your attention to something wholesome when you catch yourself daydreaming. An excellent antidote is to memorize verses of Scripture directly related to the problem—verses about lust, clean thoughts, or the devastation of illicit sex. Everytime the fantasies appear in your mind, quote a verse of Scripture and pray it back to the Lord. (By the way, this exercise can help you in any area that causes you to stumble.)

One thing to remember: When you catch yourself fantasizing, don't waste time castigating yourself. Accept the fact that you're a sinner and that sinners do these things. Rather, as soon as you realize what you're doing, thank the Lord for interrupting the fantasy, ask for His forgiveness, and then rely on His power to turn from the fantasy to the thoughts that please Him. In time, your fantasies will become less frequent and easier to resist.

Masturbation

Christian singles who struggle with the problem of masturbation many times have a terrible time trying to stop. Tremendous failure complexes can develop. God

would never want a Christian single to hurt or waste his
or her spiritual life struggling defeatedly with such a
matter. God is much more concerned that you spend
your time focusing on His gracious love and forgiveness.

To defeat the masturbation cycle in your life three facts
should be fundamentally understood. First, masturbation is a common occurrence and will not cripple or
blind you, as the old wives' tales have it. You should not
treat is as some deep, dark weakness or sickness nor let it
destroy your self-worth.

Second, the main reason Christians who desire to
please God continue to masturbate is that masturbation
becomes an emotional crutch or release. As conflicting as
it might be spiritually, masturbation brings real physical
release. Unfortunately, guilt is usually not far behind.

Third, while it would be overstating Scripture to say
masturbation is totally biblically wrong, I feel we unequivocally can say that masturbation is outside the
intent of God's purpose for creating sex. Also, the fact
that most Christians experience guilt as a result of masturbation indicates that the activity is not spiritually
beneficial (see also Rom. 14:22, 23).

The solution to the masturbation cycle (cycle because it
seems to follow a consistent pattern) is twofold. First, the
person must resist getting down on himself or herself.
Remember Satan is the accuser, not God. God convicts
when sin occurs, but He does not lead one into fits of
introspection and depression. God's role is always to
move one beyond sin of the past to forgiveness, worship, and glorification of Himself. Realize that depression because of masturbation is never from God. Confess
all sin when it occurs—even repetitive sin—and accept
God's forgiveness, confessing with your mouth that the
sin is as far from you as the east is from the west. Then
turn your eyes upon God.

The second aspect of dealing with the masturbation cycle is to take precaution to redirect your life away from this cycle. There are three steps I take people through to redirect their lives.

Step One: Begin right away to attack the emotional crutch that masturbation has become. It is like a weight problem. Many times I find overweight people eat even when they are not hungry, simply because eating sooths their emotional needs. If food is removed, depression sets in because the person is deprived emotionally. Masturbation is very similar. Only as we attack the emotional implications of masturbation will we be able to defeat it permanently. By faith we can overrule and redirect emotional crutches. Counsel and support may be necessary. (However, see Step Three.)

Step Two: Like attacking fantasies, the second step in controlling the masturbation cycle is to consciously identify the masturbation pattern. The times, places, related activities, and thought patterns should be clearly identified and tracked. Special efforts and creativity should be employed to anticipate and redirect these patterns. Scripture memory and devotional time should be employed to counter these patterns. Reading, movies, dating activities, and other thought-provoking input should also be reviewed. A last area to investigate honestly is the sinful spinoffs of the masturbation cycle. Such things as guilt, hurt, depression, and dishonesty are possible examples. God can best give wisdom as the total truth is known.

Step Three: This avenue is one that few singles want to take, because it involves making oneself accountable to another member of the Body of Christ. Scripture mentions confessing our sins one to another as a dimension of being open and honest before the Lord. Masturbation is a big problem precisely because it is so intimate and private. In 1 John, the apostle tells us the importance of walking in the light as God is in the light. Confession brings sin into the light. It can help in one's desire to stop masturbation.

Obviously, the choice of a friend who can be trusted to both keep silent and lovingly accept your struggle is the tough part of this step. A Jonathan or David type friend, a mature leader in your church, or a Christian counselor are good choices. Repeated, immediate confession dissolves improper emotional crutches and allows the other person to support you with prayer and additional insight. God's light shines freely in an atmosphere cleansed by confession.

Masturbation can be defeated without great fits of depression if all God's resources are freely available.

The sexual relationship was given by God as a blessing to married couples for reproduction. Masturbation is obviously outside God's basic purpose for sex. Therefore, I believe it is not glorifying to God (nor is it truly useful to the one who engages in it), and I would especially discourage any attitudes, ideas, or actions that encourage the practice.

Homosexuality

Recently I was talking with a Christian psychologist who confirmed what I, too, had begun to observe. More and more people are considering homosexuality to be an acceptable expression of one's sexuality. I believe this thinking will become widespread in the next ten years because of the male-female role confusion of the 1970s. The confusion and compromise concerning this subject is alarming!

Biblically speaking, homosexuality is sin. Paul stated this fact in Romans 1:26,27:

For this reason God gave them over to degrading passions; for their women exchanged the natural function for that which is unnatural, and in the same way also the men abandoned the natural function of the woman and burned in their desire toward one another, men with men committing indecent acts and receiving in their own persons the due penalty of their error.

I know there are people, even some Christians, who have tried to sidestep or explain away what Paul was saying clearly about homosexuality and lesbianism. But to do so is a grave injustice to the persons engaged in these activities. Jesus said the truth sets us free, and I believe that deep down inside each person who is living the so-called "gay" life is the desire to be free of that degrading compulsion. We hear a lot about "false guilt," but oftentimes our guilt is true guilt—*we really are wrong*. Freedom then comes only through repentance and God's forgiveness in Jesus Christ.

Although I believe homosexuality is unnatural and wrong from God's perspective, I do not believe it is always the result of a deliberate turning away from God. Many people developed homosexual tendencies as children, when they lived in environments beyond their control. Under no circumstances should we fear, ignore, or judge brothers and sisters in Christ who are burdened by this tendency. The key to our support is their agreement with God about the matter. We all have besetting sins that would be easier to resist if others were praying for us instead of condemning us.

Every single person should be aware of the growing temptations and social pressures to experiment with homosexuality. Flee any involvement in this life-sapping trap.

I believe that Satan—the father of lies—has convinced

many people that homosexuality is somehow a mystical experience. In other words, individuals who are open to sexual experimentation or who have homosexual tendencies seem to believe that there is some mystical power or force in them that cannot be controlled. In a sense this is true—the force within is called sin. The deception is the part about its being uncontrollable. As long as Satan is able to perpetuate this farce, actions based on faith in God are blocked. Single people who struggle with homosexuality often say to me, "Can I help whom I am attracted to?" Perhaps not. But one can help whether or not to allow attraction to lead to sin. Once denying the craving becomes a habit, I believe, in time, natural sexual desires and marriage can be experienced and enjoyed.

For instance, I have a tendency to be an adulterer, but I will not commit acts of adultery. In addition, I will not go through life feeling shortchanged because I did not commit adultery. I have the tendency because I am a sinner; but because I belong to Christ I am emotionally, spiritually, and *practically* free *not* to commit adultery, even though that tendency is there. What I am saying is, you don't have to sin!

I have worked with men in prisons who, before entering, would have been repulsed—even enraged—if another man had propositioned them. Yet after four or five years in prison, their minds become open to the idea of sex with another man. Tragically, if this openness leads to sexual contact, sure enough, there will be a sexual response.

One prisoner asked me if he had had a latent homosexual tendency all his life. No! He just opened himself to a sinful act and the sinful nature within him responded.

I do not intend to oversimplify a very complex problem. My point is, there is no mystery in homosexuality. There is absolute hope for the person who identifies more with Christ than with homosexuality. Sin can be controlled—even abandoned—by those who belong to the Lord Jesus. If you struggle with homosexual tendencies, be sure to seek spiritual counsel.

Adultery and Fornication

Biblically speaking, sexual intercourse outside of marriage is wrong. There is simply no way around that fact, and most single Christians know this truth—even if they don't like it. These days, though, many would rather take their chances sinning than live a celibate life. I am appalled at the number of single Christians having affairs. I want to shout, "Hey, don't you realize what you're doing to your life, to the lives of others, and to the heart of God?"

People have affairs for three reasons: (1) sexual appetite and lust, (2) society says it's okay, even normal, and (3) the need to be loved.

A single guy who was bitterly angry with God for not bringing him a wife came in deep depression to see me. In just one hour, I discovered that he had been in and out of three affairs, one with a married friend, two out of the last three years. How, may I ask, was he going to recognize a wife if God had brought her along?

Sex outside of marriage can be pleasurable—where would the temptation be if it weren't? But the pleasure is fleeting, leaving one empty, guilty, and insecure. Also, once sexually active, a person's desire for regular sex is stronger. A young woman once shared with me that she had been involved in five affairs in five years. She derived little satisfaction from these relationships, but sleeping alone, now, was almost unbearable. Had she never had sex she would have been more content and less frustrated.

Of course, there are other unavoidable consequences of having sex without benefit of marriage. Birth control methods are *never* one hundred percent effective, and the Pill and IUDs are known for certain detrimental side effects. So, what if pregnancy results? Do you go the next step and have an abortion? Or, do you choose the right, though more difficult, route and have the baby? If you're the father, do you marry a woman whom you perhaps have no love for? Do you refuse to marry but go through the pregnancy with her? Or do you run from the situation, denying your responsibility? As a Christian whose sin has led to this consequence, what do you do next?

A single person involved with a married individual is committing adultery. The consequences can range from a broken home to neglected children to a life of deception and hypocrisy. Nothing can justify the act of adultery. Destruction is its only result (see Prov. 7, especially vv. 22,23).

If you are or have been involved in an affair, my intention is not to condemn but to warn. God's forgiveness is sufficient for any sin. But *true* sorrow leads to repentance (see 2 Cor. 7:9,10), and repentance means wholeheartedly turning away from sin. Seek out a mature believer, confess your sin to him or her, and pray together for deliverance. We all need to do this more often, for the Bible commands it and promises healing as a result (see James 5:16).

Pleasure and Sensuality

A single Christian is not exempt from the pressures and influences of our hedonistic culture. That's really what we've been talking about throughout this chapter. Briefly, though, I'd like to mention three areas where the world's way of finding pleasure often attracts single people.

Drug and alcohol use has become an acceptable form of social pleasure among most people in this country. The "Happy Hour" is a popular way of attracting customers, who stop off with coworkers at their favorite lounge after work. Many Christians have come to believe that social drinking is okay, especially if they are to befriend their non-Christian colleagues. Most often, though, the real motive behind drinking, sniffing cocaine, and smoking hashish or marijuana is a rather rebellious desire to experience a new sensation—to feel "high." In essence this is the same as saying that God is not enough. We want to satisfy our senses, not our spirit.

Associated with drug and alcohol use is a whole life-style that basically thumbs its nose at God. As a Christian, I believe you cannot participate in this life-style and call Jesus Lord at the same time. Jesus ate with sinners, but He also boldly called them to repentance. He in no way compromised truth and godly behavior in order not to offend anyone. He was not afraid to be different, and therein lay His charisma.

Closely related to the alcohol and drug culture is a trap I call *"bar life."* Singles bars can be found in almost every city in this country. Loud music, swaying bodies, laughter, and the temporary comfort of being with people add up to an artificial high that resembles the effects of drugs or alcohol. Single women are hoping to meet attractive single men, and vice versa. The whole experience is superficial, based on first impressions and outward appearances. All decisions regarding the people around you are based on your senses. Do they look good, smell good, and feel good? Can they make *me* feel good? This way of thinking about others, and the life-style that says "Life is a party" is not of God. Bar-hopping and spiritual growth are incompatible.

Again, one behavior leads to another. People who pursue worldly pleasures are usually caught up in what I call *appearance worship*. Men and women who base their opinions about others on appearances only are themselves preoccupied with their own physical appearance. The culture says a woman should be sensuous and a man should be macho. Christians buy into this, and so we see Christian women wearing extremely provocative clothes, dewy makeup, sexy hairstyles, and jewelry. I really believe some women don't realize fully that they're tempting men to want to have sex with them, not to want to love and marry them. Christian men, likewise, may have their hair styled, wear clothes they think make them appear virile, drive cars that add to their image, and work out three times a week. They go to all this trouble, never realizing that most Christian women will be little impressed unless they can somehow demonstrate compassion and humility. How much time do you spend trying to *appear* desirable? What kind of person are you on the inside?

Looking one's best is certainly no sin, but carefully calculating how to attract the opposite sex by how one dresses usually leads to the wrong kind of attraction.

Don't pursue a sensuous life-style. Momentary pleasures and superficial relationships based primarily on physical attraction lead only to emptiness. Such a life lacks true meaning and eternal value.

As you read back over this chapter, remember two things. First, anyone who reads this chapter in isolation from the faith concepts in the rest of the book will not be able to understand the hope these observations bring. Do not allow these standards to discourage you; instead, ask God to give you His wisdom and approach them in the joy of pleasing Him.

Second, no single can live a godly life apart from God's grace and power. In the next chapter, we will examine how to realize God's power to live a victorious life.

14

The Power to Live Victorious Lives

"I want to be visionary in my life and in my relation-ships, but I just keep blowing it!" Singles, like married people, have a hard time living consistent Christian lives. Paul said in Romans 7:15:

> For that which I am doing, I do not understand; for I am not practicing what I would like to do, but I am doing the very thing I hate.

If the apostle Paul had a problem living the Christian life at times, surely it is not surprising that you and I do.

The Power of God's Spirit and His Forgiveness

"I feel like I'm on a roller coaster! One minute I'm up, and spiritual concepts make sense to me. Then a few days later, I'm down, and I find myself struggling with all of my old problems. I want to believe that Christianity is practical, but I don't see many Christians who are models."

Statements such as these are common. In the day of the "born again" movement, most new Christians quickly find out that becoming a Christian is not the only step necessary to becoming a successful Christian.

A number of years ago, Billy Graham estimated that

up to ninety-five percent of Christians did not know how to live the Christian life successfully. No wonder non-Christians are so critical of Christians.

Is living a Christian life really possible? Every single who hopes to apply the principles of this book must answer this question. The apostle Paul alluded to the problem in one of his letters to Timothy.

Two Life-styles

In preparing Timothy to be successful in living the Christian life, Paul talked about two life-styles. He said,

> Realize this, that in the last days difficult times will come. For men will be lovers of self, lovers of money, boastful, arrogant, revilers, disobedient to parents, ungrateful, unholy, unloving, irreconcilable, malicious gossips, without self-control, brutal, haters of good, treacherous, reckless, conceited, lovers of pleasure rather than lovers of God; holding to a form of godliness, although they have denied its power . . . (2 Tim. 3:1–4).

This explanation fits many of the life-styles and attitudes of Americans today, and unfortunately of many Christians as well.

Paul encourages Timothy to seek another life-style, "You, however, continue in the things you have learned and become convinced of . . . from childhood you have known these sacred writings which are able to give you the wisdom that leads to salvation . . . " (2 Tim. 3:14,15). These same Scriptures are available to us today.

Three Kinds of People

The apostle Paul talks a great deal in all of his writings about why some people understand God and why others do not. Paul explains that the different responses of humankind to life are tied to varying degrees of wisdom. He identifies three kinds of people.

First Paul writes,

> A *natural man* does not accept the things of the Spirit of God; for they are foolishness to him, and he cannot understand them, because they are spiritually appraised (1 Cor. 2:14, italics mine).

The natural man represents the non-Christian. Christianity is foolishness to him. He is not able to discern spiritual things. Faith, for him, is not possible. From his perspective, he is in control of his life and the world revolves around him.

Paul continues:

> But he who is *spiritual* appraises all things, yet he himself is appraised by no man (v. 15, italics mine).

The spiritual person represents the mature, wise Christian. This person understands God and faith. He or she has a second dimension: a newly created spirit. Rather than life revolving around a self-centered nature, Christ now controls the life through His Holy Spirit. The result is a godly life-style, full of wisdom.

Paul explains the conflict when he writes,

> . . . for you are still fleshly. For since there is jealousy and strife among you, are you not fleshly, and are you not walking like mere men? (1 Cor. 3:3).

The apostle gives us the key to the conflict of the two life-styles when he introduces this third kind of person: an immature Christian. The fleshly or carnal Christian, just like the non-Christian, does not discern the things of Scripture. He or she reverts to the life-style of the old nature. The difference is that the carnal person has the potential to mature and grow in understanding; the old nature cannot without Christ.

Now Billy Graham's statement begins to make sense. He was saying that ninety-five percent of all Christians are carnal, living a self-centered life just like the non-Christian. The other five percent are mature and spiritual people whose lives are characterized by God's wisdom.

Every single should identify the type of person and life-style that best describes his or her own. Scripture tells us that every person is born spiritually dead (the old nature). When one accepts the work of Christ on the cross to be united eternally with God, that person is spiritually "born again" to become a new creation. The new babe in Christ still has a self-centered nature called the flesh, but a new, spiritual life has been created. If the babe in Christ grows and matures in wisdom, then he or she will be perfected in spiritual things, living a life-style of wisdom.

Spiritual Battle

Have you ever felt a struggle going on inside you between right and wrong? Have you ever experienced urges and desires that are in opposition to one another? Throughout our lives a battle exists for the control of our will. This battle is between our self-centered flesh and God's Spirit. Since the desires of the flesh are against the desires of the Spirit, how does a person win this battle? Scripture answers this most important question emphatically. *The Holy Spirit empowers you to live the Christian life.* The Spirit of God is an equal and vital personality of the one true God. He is responsible for convicting us of sin and convincing us of what is right (see John 16:8–11).

So important is the control of the Holy Spirit, the

apostle Paul actually commands all Christians to be filled with or controlled by the Holy Spirit:

> Do not get drunk with wine, for that is dissipation, but be filled with the Spirit (Eph. 5:18).

The Greek verb for "be filled" is in the present progressive tense: "keep on being filled." The experience is repeated continually.

Every single Christian has a responsibility and a choice to let the Spirit of God control his or her life. Paul goes on to tell us that the result of being controlled with the Spirit is fulfillment. A great attitude toward others and God and an ability to give thanks in all things are just some of the results.

Confession

The basic requirement for allowing the Holy Spirit to give a person the power to live the wisdom life-style is continual fellowship with God.

In 1 John we read,

> What we have seen and also heard we proclaim to you also, that you also may have fellowship with us; and indeed our fellowship is with the Father, and with His Son Jesus Christ (1:3).

Fellowship with God is possible through His Word. However, there is a problem.

> If we say we have fellowship with Him and yet walk in the darkness [sin], we lie and do not practice the truth (v. 6).

Fellowship with God is impossible in a self-centered life-style. The power of the Holy Spirit is blocked by sin.

Confessing our sin means agreeing with God about it. He wants us to be alerted constantly when we start to turn from His life-giving way. When we agree with God about our sins immediately, we are able to release the Holy Spirit to empower us in rightful living.

Commitment to Be Filled

Christians whose lives are self-centered need to be filled with the Holy Spirit because, without Him, they are carnal. The joy and reality of the Christian life is missing on a consistent basis. Spiritual highs and lows, frustration, and powerlessness best describe their experience.

A person can experience the control of God's Spirit on a moment by moment basis if he begins the day by committing it to God's will, believing that the Holy Spirit is available to him to convict and guide. During the course of the day, if you should sin, immediately agree with God that your thought or action is sin. Based on God's Word, the sin has no more power.

After confession, believe by faith that you are filled with the Spirit, and turn to walk in a life-style pleasing to God. Because forgiveness does not involve penance or punishment, the Christian can begin to eliminate the highs and lows of the roller coaster life and see a gradual, but definite, spiritual growth pattern.

Sometimes we need to appropriate the power of the Spirit for an issue other than sin. An example would be a sudden determination to turn an area of one's life over to God. Perhaps you need special insight at work, for example, or discernment in a relationship.

In summary, remember to confess to God through prayer any known sin in your life. Thank God for forgiving you. Thank God that the Holy Spirit now controls you. These simple steps of faith release all the power of God. Praise Him, and continue to walk in the power of His Spirit.

God's Holy Spirit in the Church

Although the Holy Spirit indwells each Christian and each Christian relates to the Holy Spirit on a personal basis, it should be noted that almost every time the Holy Spirit is discussed in Scripture, the context is believers in the church. It is almost impossible for a Christian to be convicted of sin and convinced of righteousness apart from the fellowship of other believers. The Holy Spirit not only speaks personally to the believer, but He uses fellow Christians in the church to bring conviction. The power of the Spirit is tied ultimately to God's church.

Therefore, a single Christian, isolated from other believers in the Body of Christ, definitely limits God's plan and His power to work. To fully discover the power of God's Spirit, singles need to be involved in the church.

Singles, God has given us the ability to live victoriously and to stop the progress of sin in our lives. Do not pass up this opportunity to release God's power in your life through the Holy Spirit.

15

A Single's Life Goals

"I don't want to buy a home or furniture, because I'm not sure what my future wife will like."

"I know I would like that job, but I would have to get more schooling. I'm afraid doing that would cut down on my chances of getting married."

Common statements? You bet! I can relate to the rationale behind these comments because I had similar thoughts when I was single. However, I believe such thinking reflects an attitude of impermanence and perhaps of presumption. After all, it's not our place to know what the future holds. Maybe God wants you to buy a home or get more schooling *now*. I'm especially concerned about the effect of the "temporary status" mentality on the single adult's vision and success.

A positive, rewarding, and satisfying vocation, along with a personal relationship with God and a life-changing knowledge of His Word, go a long way toward producing a happy and healthy single adult who is excited about life. But too many singles settle for jobs that are not suited to their abilities, needs, and desires. Then they go home after work to little privacy, threatening roommates, and crowded space and clutter.

I continually ask singles why they are in such situations. Their answer usually is, "Where else can I go?" or "What else can I do?"

I am a strong believer in faith followed by creative action. Single Christians must stretch their creative potential and come up with alternatives that allow them the best of a permanent life-style without cutting them off from God's future leading. Singles need to settle down, to quit living in the future or second-guessing God's will ten or fifteen years down the line.

Paul wrote, "Therefore, my beloved brethen, be steadfast, immovable, always abounding in the work of the Lord, knowing that your toil is not in vain in the Lord" (1 Cor. 15:58). Nomadic-type life-styles and jobs that bring little satisfaction certainly don't breed steadfast and immovable Christians. We are not called to spontaneity but to spirituality. Singles can abound *today* in the work of the Lord and know their efforts in life are not in vain. God wants you to enjoy your state in life *now* and serve Him with a whole heart.

There are three major aims or goals I believe each single person should keep in mind if a significant life is desired. First, single Christians, as do all believers, need to determine that *God and His Word* are essential to life and must be obeyed. Obedience to God leads to caring, healthy relationships in the Body of Christ and a servant's attitude toward others, which in turn leads to further growth. Second, singles should align their *vocational activities* with their call to a life of godliness and with the gifts God has given them. Third, single people need to establish a *home*, a place of permanence with an atmosphere of security, happiness, and hospitality.

Life Goal #1: A Knowledge of God and His Word

Larry had asked me to counsel him concerning his life goals. After discussing his personal history during the first session, Larry was back the next week to hear my suggestions.

At the very top of my list was the exhortation: Place a strong emphasis on learning Scripture! Over the years I have observed many blank looks, but none compared with the expression on the face of this young man. His stare told me he couldn't believe what he had just heard.

Becoming knowledgeable in the Bible is one of the two or three most important steps any individual can make to insure a successful life. Yet many singles, when they hear this advice, think, *Here comes the traditional appeal. If that's all he has to offer concerning life goals, I'll go elsewhere.*

Let me ask you: As a single, are you not looking for a deep sense of self-worth? Are you not fighting for diversity of self-expression? Do you not desire to have others need and look to you as a knowledgable source of wisdom concerning life? Only the Holy Scriptures can open these aspects of life to you on a consistent basis. I know personally that what wisdom I have to offer others is straight from Scripture, the written Word of God.

"Let the word of Christ richly dwell within you, with all wisdom teaching and admonishing one another with psalms and hymns and spiritual songs, singing with thankfulness in your heart to God" (Col. 3:16) is Paul's repeated exhortation. One who allows God's Word to dwell richly in his heart and mind, and who shares the Word with others, will be balanced in his understanding of the Christian faith and of the world around him as well. Consider these practical, even "old-fashioned," reasons to learn God's Word.

Faith

Throughout this book we have discussed two courses

of life. One is to follow one's human instincts in every situation. The other course involves subjecting human instinct to God's perspective. This latter course is called faith—doing something God has said, even when it contradicts our human instinct. Only faith can take one out of the natural realm and enable one to have and maintain growing, lasting relationships. Therefore, faith is vital to any individual who desires to live a purposeful life.

How do we develop the ability to live by faith? The apostle emphatically responds, "So faith comes from hearing, and hearing by the word of Christ" (Rom. 10:17). Our means to faith is holy Scripture.

The more you know and act on Scripture, the stronger your faith becomes. Self-worth, ways to develop relationships and show our concern for others, vocational direction, discipleship pointers, and literally every possible need and desire in life requires that we know Scripture if we expect to succeed. Nothing could be more practical. Joshua says it well:

> "This book of the law shall not depart from your mouth, but you shall meditate on it day and night, so that you may be careful to do according to all that is written in it; for then you will make *your way prosperous*, and then *you will have success*" (Josh. 1:8, italics mine).

Direction

Every interest and desire I've had in life initially required me to ask the question, "How do I do it?" Beyond the exciting dimension of faith, Scripture also contains down-to-earth, practical directions for living life. After just a year of marriage, for example, I realized that I did not know how to succeed in marriage. But I *desired* to know how to succeed. Scripture provided the "how to's" I needed. Desire requires knowledge before fulfillment is possible.

My question to you is, have you really considered putting Scripture at the top of your "how to" list? Scripture contains more practical information than libraries could ever hold!

Self-Worth

As said earlier, advertisers have one goal: to create a sense of dissatisfaction within us in regard to who we are and what we have. Add to the effects of advertising our natural instinct to compare ourselves with others, and the result is often a self-worth crisis.

What is self-worth? Simply, it is being valuable to God, to yourself, and to others. I am never "down on myself" when people I truly respect are communicating love and appreciation for me. The broader and more diversified this respect, the more self-confidence I feel.

God, in a number of places in Scripture, commands men and women to do such things as rule, keep, reign, love, reproduce, reflect, disciple, teach, and counsel. The implication is that people have been equipped and need to be involved with others in these ways to experience fulfillment. Self-image is enhanced by one's sense of productivity. What better opens the door for you to a sense of value and productivity in life?

Listen: Scripture helps open the door! Because of my knowledge of Scripture, I am equipped to offer counsel, to teach, to develop faithful relationships—all ways to serve others and demonstrate God's love. Knowledge of the Word translates into personal development and Christian maturity.

Life Goal # 2: A Challenging Vocation

Single men and women spend about one third of their time at work. That fact alone means that finding the right vocation is important. Personal pride, a sense of value and productivity, and satisfaction with life are to a large extent dependent on job contentment.

For many, vocational satisfaction is an elusive goal. Many people reach mid-life wishing they had picked another field of endeavor. Popular jobs are hard to come by, while less popular jobs barely keep up with inflation and often are boring and unchallenging. A fulfilling vocational life can easily become a hit or miss situation.

Paul, as a single man, was confident at the end of his life (and during his life, for that matter) that he had been directed by God. He was certain he had finished his mission. His certainty of completing the course God had marked out for him was simply a result of his obedience to God's calling. Knowing God's will—and doing it—opens entirely new avenues of accomplishment concerning work. Doing what God wants eliminates having to say, "I wish I'd done something else with my life."

Far too many people settle for vocational situations not suitable to their strengths, abilities, and desires. The reason? Most of us do not explore fully God's wisdom concerning our calling in life. What are some of the ways you can determine the will of God for your vocation? Here are some guidelines.

1. What do you really *like* to do? The psalmist says the Lord gives us the desires of our hearts (see Ps. 37:4). Seek what you enjoy!

2. The leaders in your church are there to help you. Talk the possibilities through with them.

3. In Genesis 3 God established that man would toil

with sweat on his face in order to eat. Since that time, and because of sin, *laziness* has been a destructive force. People are happiest when they work hard. Therefore, a satisfying job is one that requires toil and hard work. If you aren't working hard, something needs to be reevaluated.

4. Beyond this, what do you do *well*? Each of us is gifted in some way. We all know that when we work at jobs that require our gifts, we accomplish our tasks with satisfaction. Therefore, it is important to know our spiritual gifts. Paul says, "Now concerning spiritual gifts, brethren, I do not want you to be unaware" (1 Cor. 12:1). Gifts are given to contribute to the overall welfare of Christ's church, but they also have application vocationally. Emphasize them in job selection. Again, your church should be able to confirm your gifts with you.

(The fact that God gave all Christians spiritual gifts and that He gave each member of the church an individual contribution to make indicates to me that each believer has a specific ministry tied to spiritual gifts. Some may have a public ministry. Others may have gifts to contribute behind the scenes. For Paul, his ministry of preaching was primary, and tent-making, his vocation, was supportive. The reverse is true for us more times than not. But God views both the tent-making and the ministry as a well-blended course over a lifetime.)

5. Viewing one's job as *from* God is essential. With such an attitude, job pressure drops, performance improves, and one's sense of responsibility increases. On the other hand, if you ask God to provide you with work, you will be protected from certain jobs because of obvious conflicts with God and His Word. The Scriptures teach that whatever we do, we are to do it for the glory of God (see 1 Cor. 10:31).

6. The end result should be peace and satisfaction for both the employer and employee. Job complacency is not an option for a Christian, and being passive has no part in our vocational life. Biding one's time is destructive.

7. Be creative. Look at several vocations and compare them to make sure that your being single will not limit advancement. You may even prayerfully consider starting your own company, drawing other gifted people together to form a vibrant business partnership. If you have a desire to go back to school, and finances permit, that could be an option. Consider the callings of pastor, counselor, teacher, if God opens the door.

God has a vital purpose for every Christian. One's job may fulfill that purpose directly or it may support you financially as you pursue the ministry to which God has called you. There is no limit to the opportunities open to single people. And remember: God responds to your faith!

Life Goal # 3: Establishing a Home

I remember well an evening several years ago when I had dinner with some single friends. As you know, four men living together in one apartment is not always a pretty sight! The subtle gymnasium smell subsided after a few minutes, but then I had a sneaking suspicion that the plate I was eating on had not been washed properly. These men always looked clean and sharp, so I never dreamed this was the kind of situation they lived in.

I should never have gone into the kitchen. But it was the polite thing to do, after all, to help clear the table. Tennis shoes were in the microwave oven (an excellent way to dry them, I was told). As I put the butter dish back into the refrigerator, I observed a half-eaten apple and a piece of bread that must have been there at least a month!

Many single people live in some of the most *unbelievable* situations. I know these men well enough to know that their mothers would have died instantly if they had seen the mess they lived in. Certainly, not all singles are messy—not by a long shot. But many of the single people I know live in situations that they in no way think of as "home" in any permanent sense.

Everyone ought to be able to think of the place where they eat and sleep as *home*. An orderly, attractive living environment offers peace and privacy, as well as a place to entertain others in a way that makes them, too, feel at home. Don't put off buying furniture (it need not be expensive) and other necessary items. Be creative as you decorate your home—express yourself! Make your living situation *your* home, as if you will live there for many years.

Roommates/Housemates

Of course, you may choose to have roommates. This should be entered into with much prayer. You need to be sure God is calling you to this arrangement, (you may want to read over the principles discussed in Part II for faith relationships). Mainly you need to be ready to think in terms of *our* home when two or three dwell together.

A word of caution: Christians should not, in my opinion, consider sharing living quarters with non-Christians, at least not on a long-term basis (for instance, if you are in or return to college, you may not have a choice). The inevitable frictions would put a strain on such a friendship, and your "home" would become a mission field instead of a haven.

Communicate well with potential roommates *before* making a commitment. Discuss personal habits, finances, dating patterns, spiritual interest, and anything you want to know about the potential roommate. Discuss commitment and past problems and conflicts with other roommates. If your potential roommate has a history of past conflicts with other roommates, be careful—especially if he or she blames these conflicts entirely on his or her former roommates.

Realize that each roommate relationship can be a significant way for God to meet your needs and to help perfect you into the likeness of Christ. Often it is easier to live alone, to hide from commitment and communication. But it also is easy to miss the value a roommate relationship can add.

I believe there does come a time when a single person may want to live alone. For instance, two or three women living together may be unreasonable if they each own their own living room furniture and enjoy managing their own household. Without meaning to stereotype women, I think it's generally true that they enjoy expressing themselves by the way they decorate their home and show hospitality to others. Obviously, two women living together cannot each run the household fully. Each will have to sacrifice her desires from time to time if harmony is to result. Two or more women trying to manage the same household isn't often practical. Likewise, a single man may want to own his own house and furnish it to his own liking. Not many of us would expect a forty-year-old bachelor to have a roommate. However, if singles live alone, they should make special efforts to establish and maintain commitment or covenant relationships elsewhere.

Personal Enjoyment

As part of your home life, do you have a plan for developing personal happiness—and your sense of humor? Many singles are overly active and yet are not having fun in life. Our serious, pressured life-styles can squeeze enjoyment from our daily routines. Last year, I simply assigned one single woman to laugh out loud twice a day for a month. The results were amazing! She had forgotten how to laugh. But even worse, her friends had forgotten she could.

The older people get, the less they are willing to try to be lighthearted. Fun is painful—in the sense that it requires venturing into new things. The results, however, are worth whatever uncomfortableness you may experience.

Begin with redoing activities you have enjoyed in the past. Pick up any talents and abilities you began and enjoyed as a child, for example, and develop them. Hobbies and athletic activities offer great job and relational experiences. Cultural events open unbelievable opportunities for new enjoyment. Plays, concerts, opera, ballet, and art shows are just the beginning of an endless array of enjoyable activities.

Travel is an excellent opportunity to enjoy new and stimulating sights and experiences. Today a single person can literally see the world. Check for airline deals and vacation packages with a travel agency. Travel, prayerfully planned, can be reasonable in cost and a great deal of fun. Few activities add more to a person's life than a trip with a friend. Plan short weekend trips, including a nice place to stay, sightseeing, and special eating places. Or arrange an inexpensive camping trip with a group. Take time to leave your responsibilities behind for a break that will give you new energy and vitality by the time you return.

Knowledge of Scripture, the right vocation, and an enjoyable living situation are all necessary elements of a purposeful life. These in conjunction with an intimate knowledge of God, faith relationships, and integral, God-given service within the church allow a person to experience life at its best in this world.

Please don't settle for a life of waiting, putting off, and being discontent. Begin to live—*now*!

Epilogue

My greatest desire is that you would not wait for marriage, as Debbie did, or for anything for that matter, but that you would realize that because of God's faithfulness, there is nothing to wait for! I want you to know and trust that *everything* pertaining to life and godliness is truly in a knowledge of God . . . to believe life begins and *is* today! Everything you need is available *now*.

Having believed and trusted in almighty God, I would exhort singles everywhere to recognize God's provision of His church for their needs and then receive and wrap themselves in the arms of God's love—arms that are provided by Him in the person of their fellow brothers and sisters in Christ.

My prayer is that you will be released to live a purposeful, daring life of faith as you fully commit yourself to seeking God and being a part of His family. My prayer is for a life in which your gifts and aspirations will be limitlessly used and appreciated—a life of significance, authority, and love in which you can honestly say at life's end, "I have fought the good fight, I have finished the course, I have kept the faith."